PRINCIPLES OF MANAGEMENT

PRINCIPLES OF MANAGEMENT

By

G. MURUGESAN

Asst. Professor
Deptt. of Management Studies
V.M.K.V. Engineering College
Salem
Tamil Nadu

UNIVERSITY SCIENCE PRESS

(An Imprint of Laxmi Publications Pvt. Ltd.)

BANGALORE • CHENNAI • COCHIN • GUWAHATI • HYDERABAD
JALANDHAR • KOLKATA • LUCKNOW • MUMBAI • RANCHI
NEW DELHI

Published by :

UNIVERSITY SCIENCE PRESS

(*An Imprint of Laxmi Publications Pvt. Ltd.*)

113, Golden House, Daryaganj,
New Delhi-110002

Phone : 011-43 53 25 00
Fax : 011-43 53 25 28

www.laxmipublications.com
info@laxmipublications.com

First Edition : 2012

OFFICES

© **Bangalore**	080-26 75 69 30	© **Kolkata**	033-22 27 43 84
© **Chennai**	044-24 34 47 26	© **Lucknow**	0522-220 99 16
© **Cochin**	0484-237 70 04, 405 13 03	© **Mumbai**	022-24 91 54 15, 24 92 78 69
© **Guwahati**	0361-251 36 69, 251 38 81	© **Patna**	0612-230 00 97
© **Hyderabad**	040-24 65 23 33	© **Ranchi**	0651-221 47 64
© **Jalandhar**	0181-222 12 72		

UPM-9540-090-PRINCIPLES OF MANAG-MUR **C—**

Typeset at : Goswami Associates, Delhi.

CONTENTS

PREFACE

Principles of Management is a paper to commerce and management students. This book covers the syllabi of all the Indian Universities at the maximum. This book is written from the point of view of students in simple language. The concept of management is explained in a detailed manner. The subject matter of this book has been collected from authentic literature. With a view to facilitating proper understanding of concepts, the concepts are defined with the help of a large number of definitions. Eminent author's comments are incorporated in appropriate places throughout this book.

A good book is free from technical and uncommon words as far as possible. Block letters are used to differentiate the point from the explanation. The author will be very thankful to readers if they offer constructive suggestions for improvement of this book.

—Author

Chapter 1 BASICS OF MANAGEMENT

1.1. INTRODUCTION TO MANAGEMENT

The managers achieve organizational objectives by getting work from others and not performing in the tasks themselves.

Management is an art and science of getting work done through people. It is the process of giving direction and controlling the various activities of the people to achieve the objectives of an organization.

1.2. DEFINITION OF MANAGEMENT

There are numerous definitions of management. Different experts have defined different points of view.

*According to Mary Parker Follett, **"Management is the art of getting things done through people."***

*Harold Koontz defined as, **"Management is the art of getting things done through and with people in formally organized groups. It is the art of creating an environment in which people can perform and individuals could cooperate towards attaining of group goals."***

*In view of Joseph Massie, **"Management is defined as the process by which a cooperative group directs actions towards common goals."***

*George.R.Terry's point of view, **"Management is a distinct process, consisting of planning, organizing, actuating and controlling, performed to determine and accomplish stated goals by the use of human beings and other resources."***

According to this definition, management is a process a systematic way of doing things. The four management functions included in this process are planning, organizing, directing and controlling.

Planning refers manager's think of their actions in advance. Their actions are usually based on some method, plan or logic, rather than on a hunch.

Organizing refers manager's coordinate the human and material resources of the organization.

Actuating refers managers motivate and direct subordinates

Controlling refers attempts to ensure that there is no deviation from the plan or norms.

This definition also indicates that managers use people and other resources such as finance, equipment's etc. in attaining their goals.

Finally, the definition states that the management involves the act of achieving the organization's objectives. These objectives will, of course, vary with each organization.

The following chart clearly presents this definition of management.

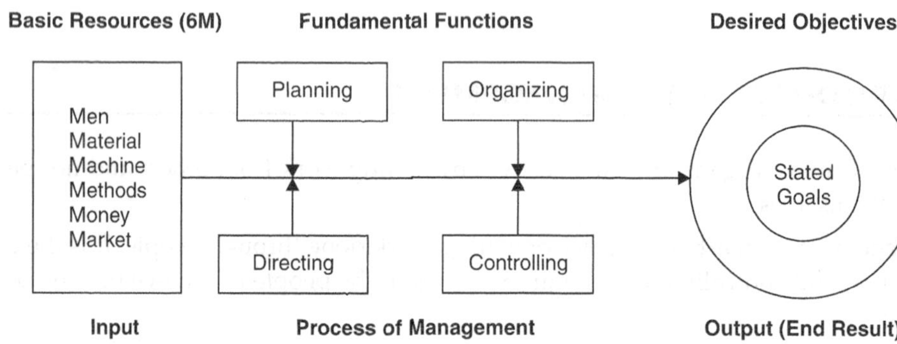

1.3. NATURE/CHARACTERISTICS OF MANAGEMENT

Following are the nature and characteristics of Management

1. **Management is an activity.** It is a process of organized activity concerned with efficient utilization of resources of production like men, material, machine, money etc.
2. **Management is a purposeful activity.** It is concerned with the achievement of an objective through its functions. Objectives may be explicit or implicit.
3. **Management concerned with the efforts of a group.** Management is concerned with management of people and not the direction of things. It motivates the workers to contribute their best.
4. **Management is getting things done.** A manager does not do any operating work himself but gets it done through others.
5. **Management applies economic principles.** Management is the art of applying the economic principles that underlie a control of men and materials in the enterprise under consideration.

6. **Management involves decision-making.** It is a decision-making process and the decisions are involved in all the functions of management.
7. **Management coordinates all activities and resources.** It is concerned with coordination of all activities and resources to attain the specific objectives.
8. **Management is a universal activity.** The techniques and tools of management are universally applicable.
9. **Management is an integrating process.** It integrates the men, materials and machines for achieving stated objectives.
10. **Management is concerned with direction and control.** It is concerned with direction and control of human efforts to attain the specific objectives.
11. **Management is intangible.** It is abstract and cannot be seen. It is evidenced by the quality of organization and through its results.
12. **Management is both science and an art.** Management has certain universally applicable principles, laws etc. Hence, it is a science. It is also an art, because it is concerned with application of knowledge for the solution of organizational problems.
13. **Management is a profession.** It is becoming a profession because there is established principles of management which being applied in practice.
14. **Management is an inter-disciplinary approach.** Management as a body of discipline takes the help or other social science like psychology, sociology, engineering, economics, mathematics etc.
15. **Management is dynamic and not static.** Management adopts itself to the social changes and also introduces innovation in methodology.

1.4. SCOPE OF MANAGEMENT

The scope of management is very wide. The functional areas of management may be classified into the following categories.

(*i*) Production Management

(*ii*) Marketing Management

(*iii*) Financial Management

(*iv*) Personnel Management

(*i*) **Production Management.** *Production function so as to produce the right goods in right quantity at the right time and at the right cost.* It consists of the following activities.

- Designing the product
- Location and layout of plant and building
- Operations of purchase and storage of materials
- Planning and control of factory operations
- Repairs and maintenance

- Inventory control and quality control
- Research and development etc.

(*ii*) **Marketing Management.** ***It refers to the identification of consumer's needs and supplying them the goods and services, which can satisfy those, wants.*** The activities are as follows:

- Marketing Research to determine the needs and expectations of consumers
- Planning and developing suitable products
- Setting appropriate prices
- Selecting the right channels of distribution
- Promotional activities like advertising and salesmanship to communicate with the customers.

(*iii*) **Financial Management.** ***Financial management seeks to ensure the right amount and type of funds to business at the right time and at reasonable cost.*** The activities are as follows:

- Estimate the volume of funds requires for long term and short term needs of business
- Selecting the appropriate sources of funds
- Raising the required funds at the right time
- Ensuring proper utilization and allocation of raised funds
- Administration of earnings.

(*iv*) **Personnel Management.** ***It involves planning, organizing, directing and controlling the procurement, development, compensation, maintenance etc. of the human resources in an enterprise.*** It consists of the following activities:

- Manpower planning
- Recruitment
- Selection
- Training and Development
- Performance Appraisal
- Compensation and promotion
- Employee services and benefits
- Maintaining personnel records etc.

1.5. FUNCTIONS OF MANAGEMENT

Different authors offering different names for the same functions of management

Henri Fayol identifies five functions of management viz, *planning, organizing, commanding, coordinating and controlling.*

Koontz and O'Donnell, divides the management functions into *planning, organizing, staffing, directing and controlling.*

Warren Haynes and Joseph Massie classifies management functions into decision-making, planning, organizing, staffing, directing, controlling, and communicating.

Luther Gulick, states seven such functions under the catch word **"POSDCORB"**

Which stand for

P – Planning
O – Organizing
S – Staffing
D – Directing
Co – Coordinating
R – Reporting
B – Budgeting

As per managers are concerned, the following five functions are essential. They are Planning, Organizing, Staffing, Directing, and Controlling. In addition to above five functions, the two functions such as Innovations and representation are also necessary for managers.

1.6. MANAGEMENT PROCESS

There is enough disagreement among management writers on the classification of managerial functions. Some classify these functions into four types, some into six or seven. The terminology is also not always alike, different authors offering different names for the same functions of management. **For managerial purpose, the following five functions are very essential for managers. They are planning, organizing, staffing, directing and controlling.**

(*i*) **Planning.** ***Planning is the function that determines in advance what should be done. It is looking ahead and preparing for the future. It is a process of deciding the business objectives and charting out the methods of attaining those objectives. In other words, it is the determination of what is to be done, how and where it is to be done, who is to do it and how results are to be evaluated.*** This is done not only for the organization as a whole but for every division or department or sub-unit of the organization. It is a function, which is performed by managers at all levels, like top, middle and supervisory levels of management. Plans made by top management of the organizations whole may cover periods as long as five or ten years. Also, plans made by middle or first line managers, cover such shorter periods. Such plans may be for the next days or weeks, or months, etc. for example, for a two-hour meeting to take place in a week.

Following are the sub functions of planning: forecasting, decision-making, strategic formulation, policy-making, programming, scheduling, budgeting, problem solving, innovation and research activities.

(*ii*) **Organizing.** ***It refers to coordinate human resources with other resources such as material, machine, money etc. Once managers have established objectives and developed plans to achieve them, they must design and develop a human organization that will be able to carry out those plans successfully.*** According to Allen, this organization refers to the "Structure which results from identifying and grouping work, defining and delegating responsibility and authority, and establishing relationships." According to Amitai Etzioni, "An organization is a social unit or human grouping, deliberately structured for the purpose of attaining specific goals".

The process of organizing involves the followings:

- *Identifying the activities necessary to achieve the objectives.*
- *Grouping activities into various departments.*
- *Assigning duties or tasks to appropriate individuals.*
- *Delegating necessary authority to individuals and fixing responsibilities for results.*
- *Defining authority and responsibility relationship among individuals.*

Sub-functions of organizing functions are as follows: Functionalisation, divisionalisation, departmentation, delegation, decentralization, activity analysis,task allocation.

(*iii*) **Staffing.** Staffing may also be considered an important function involved in building the human organization. ***In staffing, the manager attempts to find the right person for each job. Staffing fixes a manager's responsibility to recruit and to make certain that there is enough manpower available to fill the various positions needed in the organization. Staffing involves the selection and training of future managers and a suitable system of compensation.*** Staffing obviously cannot be done once and for all, since people are continually leaving, getting fired, retiring and dying. Often too, the changes in the organization create new positions, and these must be filled.

According to Koontz and O'Donnell, "The managerial function of staffing involves manning the organizational structure through proper and effective selection, appraisal and development of personnel to fill the roles designed into the structure".

Staffing function has the following sub functions. They are manpower planning, recruitment, selection, training and development, placement, compensation, promotion, appraisal etc.

(*iv*) **Directing.** After plans have been made and the organization has been established and staffed, the next step is to move towards its defined objectives. ***This function can be called by various names: 'Leading', 'Directing', 'Motivating', 'Actuating',*** and so on. But whatever the name used to identify it, in carrying out this function ***the manager explains to his people what they have to do and helps them do it to the best of their ability.***

Directing thus involves three sub-functions. They are as follows

- ***Communication,***
- ***Leadership and***
- ***Motivation.***

- *Communication is the process of passing information and understanding from one person to another.*
- *Leadership is the process by which a manager guides and influences the work of his subordinates.*
- *Motivation means arousing desire in the minds of workers to give their best to the enterprise. It is the act of stimulating or inspiring workers. If the workers of an enterprise are properly motivated they will pull their weight effectively, give their loyalty to the enterprise, and carry out their task effectively.*

Two broad categories of motivation are financial and non-financial. Financial motivation takes the form of salary, bonus, profit sharing, etc., while non-financial motivation takes the form of job security, opportunity of advancement, recognition, praise, etc.

(*v*) **Controlling.** ***The manager must ensure that everything occurs in conformity with the plans adopted, the instructions issued and the principles established.***

Three elements are involved in the controlling function.

- *Establishing standards of performance.*
- *Measuring current performance and comparing it against the established standards.*
- *Taking action to correct any performance that does not meet those standards. In the absence of sound control, there is no guarantee that the objectives, which have been set, will be realized. The management may go on committing mistakes without knowing them. Control compels events to conform to plans.*

Controlling function has the following sub functions. They are

- ***Fixation of standards,***
- ***Recording,***
- ***Measurement,***
- ***Reporting,***
- ***Corrective action.***

1.7. LEVELS OF MANAGEMENT

In every company, there is a managerial hierarchy or chain of command, which consists of several levels of authority. The number of management levels may differ from company to company. In a big company the management levels may be classified into three categories viz.

(*i*) Top management

(*ii*) Middle management

(*iii*) Supervisory or Operating management

In a very large enterprise the middle management levels may be subdivided into upper middle management and lower middle management

(*i*) **Top Management.** ***Top management consists of the board of Directors and the chief executives. Chief executives may be an individual, for example, Managing Director, General Manager etc., or a group of chairman and functional executive Directors.*** Board of directors is accountable to the shareholders in the annual general meetings of the company. The chief executive is concerned with the overall management of the company's operations. He maintains coordination among different departments/sections of the company. He also keeps the organizations in harmony with its external environment.

Functions

- ***To analyse and interpret changes in the external environment of the company***
- ***To establish long term corporate plans (goals, policies and strategies) of the company***

- *To formulate and approve the master budget and departmental budgets*
- *To design board organization structure*
- *To appoint departmental heads and key executives*
- *To provide overall direction and leadership to the company*
- *To represent the company to the outside world*
- *To decide the distribution of profits.*

(*ii*) **Middle Management**

(*a*) **Intermediate Management.** *Intermediate/upper middle management comprises departmental or divisional heads. For example, Marketing Manager, Production Manager, etc. It is also known as departmental or functional Management.* Each divisional or departmental heads are the overall incharge of their respective division/department. He performs the usual managerial functions of planning, organizing, staffing, directing, and controlling in relation to one department.

(*b*) **Lower middle Management.** *Lower middle management levels consist of sectional heads. For example, plant manager, sales manager, branch manager etc.* These executives serve as a link between intermediate or top management and the operating management.

Functions of Middle Management

- *To interpret and explain the plans and policies formulated by top management*
- *To monitor and control the operating performance*
- *To train, motivate and develop supervisory personnel*
- *To lay down rules and regulations to be followed by supervisory personnel.*

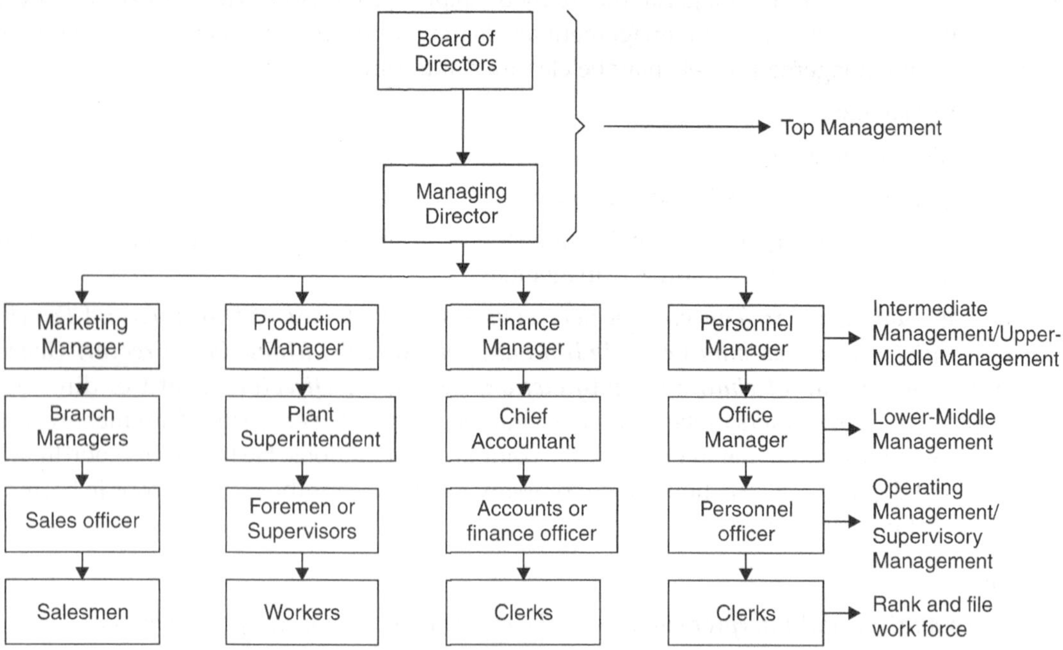

Levels of Management

(*iii*) **Supervisory/Operating Management.** This is the lowest or first level of management in an organization. ***It consists of supervisors, foremen, sales officers, accounts officer, purchase officer etc.*** They maintain close contacts with the ranks and white colour workers and supervise day-to-day operations. They serve as the channel of communication between management and the workforce. They are concerned with the mechanics of jobs.

Functions

- ***To plan day-to-day production within goals laid down by higher officials***
- ***To assign jobs to workers and to make arrangements for their training and development***
- ***To issue orders and instructions***
- ***To supervise and control workers' operations and to maintain personal contact with them***
- ***To arrange materials and tools and to maintain machinery***
- ***To advise and assist workers by explaining work procedures, solving their problems***
- ***To maintain discipline and good human relations among workers***
- ***To report feedback information and workers' problems to the higher authorities.***

1.8. SKILLS OF MANAGERS

By managerial skills, we mean the skills or qualities desired in managers, the possession of which would enable to act as practicing managers. Following three broad types of managerial skills are very essential for managers.

(*i*) Technical skills

(*ii*) Human skill or Behavioural skills

(*iii*) Conceptual skills

(*i*) **Technical Skills.** Technical skills refer to the skill and knowledge, which is required for performing an operational activity, in the best manner. *i.e.*, technical skill might be termed as technical expertise.

Technical skill is an imperative skill for managers at the lower level of management; because it is actually these people who guide and supervise work operators under their subordination. For example, mechanics work with tools, and their supervisors should have the ability to teach them how to use these tools. Similarly, the teacher, who, before, imparting teaching to pupils in a particular discipline, must be an expert in that discipline.

Technical skill is also required in managers at upper and middle levels of management. Managers at these levels do the fundamental planning for operational work leaving the detailed day-to-day operational plans to be made by the supervisory level.

(*ii*) **Human Skills or Behavioural Skills.** The basic responsibility of every manager is to get things done by others. In this process, managers need human skills. ***Human skills refer to those abilities, which are needed by the manager to effectively deal with subordinates. To manage, he has to understand their needs, interests and values. He interacts with them, guides, directs, leads,***

and motivates them. In this regard, he is expected to know general tendencies of human behaviour and factors influencing it. By using human skills, he may establish good rapport, warmth relationships and conductive interpersonal relations with his subordinates. It is needed for providing dynamic and effective leadership and building a team spirit among employees.

Since, managers at all levels in the enterprise are supposed to deal with human beings in a subordinate position; all managers from the top to the lowest levels in the management hierarchy equally need human skill.

(*iii*) **Conceptual Skills.** Conceptual skill comprise the ability to see the whole organization and the inter relationships between its parts. ***These skills refer to the ability to visualize the entire picture or to consider a situation in its totality.*** Such skills help the manager to conceptualize the environment, to analyse the forces working in a situation and to take a broad and farsighted view of the organization. Conceptual skills also include the competence to understand a problem in all its aspects to use original thinking in solving the problem. Such competence is necessary for rational decision-making.

Conceptual skill is imperative for top management level, necessary for the middle management and desirable for the lower level of management.

Thus, Technical skills deal with jobs, Human skill with persons and Conceptual skills with ideas. These types of skills are interrelated. The relative importance of these skills may differ at various levels in the organization hierarchy. Following figure is clearly explained the importance of skills required at various levels of management.

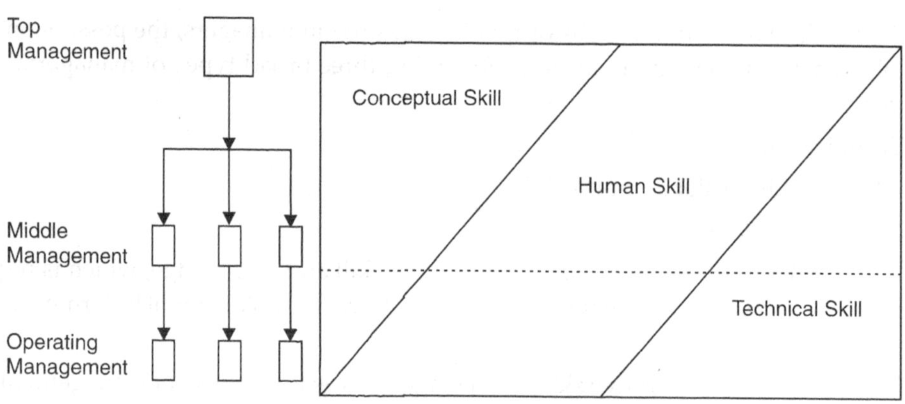

Managerial Skills at Various Levels of Management

1.9. ROLE OF MANAGERS

The job of a modern manager is very complex and multi-dimensional. *Mintzberg* has identified ten roles of a manager which are grouped into three categories viz.,

Interpersonal Roles

- Figure head

- Leader
- Liaison

Informational Roles

- Monitor
- Disseminator
- Spokesman

Decisional Roles

- Entrepreneur
- Disturbance handler
- Resource allocator
- Negotiator

1. Figure head

In this role a manager performs symbolic duties required by the status of his office. Making speeches, bestowing honours, welcoming official visitors, distributing gifts to retiring employees are examples of such ceremonial and social duties.

2. Leader

This role defines the manager relationship with his own subordinates. The manager sets an example, legitimizes the power of subordinates and brings their needs in accord with those of his organization.

3. Liaison

It describes a manager's relationship with the outsiders. A manager maintain mutually beneficial relation with other organizations, governments, industry groups, etc.

4. Monitor

It implies seeking and receiving information about his organization and external events. An example is picking up rumors about his organization.

5. Disseminator

It involves transmitting information and judgments to the members of the organization. The information relates to internal operations and the external environment. A manager calling a staff meeting after a business trip is an example of such a role.

6. Spokesman

In this role, a manager speaks for his organization. He lobbies and defends his enterprise. A manager addressing the trade union is an example.

7. Entrepreneur

It involves initiating change or acting as a change agent. For example, a manager decides to launch a feasibility study for setting up a new plant.

8. Disturbance handler

This refers to taking charge when the organization faces a problem or crisis. For example, a strike, a feud between subordinates loss of an important customer. A manager handles conflicts, complaints and competitive actions.

9. Resource allocator

In this role a manager approves budgets and schedules, sets priorities and distributes resources.

10. Negotiator

As a negotiator, a manager bargain with suppliers, dealers, trade union, agents, etc. For example, the manager may negotiate with the union leaders regarding strike issues.

1.10. EVOLUTION OF MANAGEMENT THOUGHT

To get proper and balanced perspective of theory and practice of management, all developments taking place since the beginning of the 20th century may be placed under three main categories. They are as follows:

- *Classical or traditional Management approach*
- *Behavioral or neo-classical approach*
- *Modern approach to management*

1.10.1. Classical or Traditional Management Approach

The classical approach to management is one of the oldest and most popular, known as the traditional or universal process. It is based on the assumption that the objective of an organization may vary from one to another but the management of all organizations requires similar management process. ***It has its roots in the basic concepts of division of labour and specialization. This approach consists mainly of scientific management developed by F.W.Taylor, administrative theory of management by Henry Fayol and bureaucratic organization by Max Weber.***

1.10.1.1. Theory of Scientific Management

Though scientific management theory is based on the contributions of many scholars and practitioners like Fredrick Winslow Taylor, Henry Gantt, Frank Gilbrith, Emerson and Carl Berth, etc. But F.W.Taylor has given a concrete shape to the theory of scientific management.

Taylor's Theory of Scientific Management

F.W.Taylor (1856 – 1915) is known as the ***"father of Scientific Management"***. He joined as a mechanic at midvale steel company in U.S.A at 1878. He became chief engineer in the year 1884 in the same company. During his career spanning a period of 26 years, he conducted a series of experiments in three companies: Midvale Steel, Simonds Rolling Machine and Bethlehem steel companies. While serving as a Chief Engineer of Midvale Steel Company, Taylor made several important contributions, which are classified under scientific management.

Taylor's approach aims at increasing the operational efficiency of workers by solving their work related problems, reducing in efficiency and wastage, improving their relation with management, and developing a best way of doing things. Taylor expressed the basic philosophy of scientific management in the following terms:

- ***Science, not rule of thumb:*** For solving problems and making decisions, the manager should adopt scientific attitude and use scientific thinking and methods. The 'rule of thumb' or 'Hit or miss' approach should be replaced.
- ***Harmony, not discord:*** All the departments and workers are a part of an organization. There should be complete harmony or coordination in their functioning and any kind of clash or conflict should not be allowed to crop in and, if it arises, should be reduced to a minimum.
- ***Cooperation, not individualism:*** Instead of fostering individualism, importance of cooperative group efforts should be recognised. Because, organizational objectives depends upon the group efforts not for individuals.
- ***Maximum, not restricted output:*** Production should be carried out up to the maximum capacity available in a unit.
- ***Development of each man to his greater efficiency and prosperity:*** For the prosperity of individual workers as well as the organization, the efficiency level of workers should be increased by providing scientific training and developing their potential abilities to the maximum.

Taylor based on his experience at the shop floor, developed guidelines to the practice of management as under.

(1) Scientific study and planning of work

Taylor has suggested that the work to be assigned to and performed by workers should be studied, analyzed and planned as to determine the day's fair work (standard of work) for each worker. In relation to work, following studies should be conducted to the workers on what is to be done and how it can be done, efficiently.

(*i*) **Work study.** The object of work-study is to improve efficiency. Efficiency could be improved and increased by expending fewer resources and reaping greater returns.

(*ii*) **Motion study.** The object of motion study is to identify and eliminate unnecessary, avoidable and wasteful movements and motions of men and machines. These movements and motions are closely watched and recorded. On the basis of this study it can be determined whether the movements and motions are productive or incidental or unproductive.

(*iii*) **Time study.** It is popularly known as work measurement. It is basically concerned with productivity. The exact time required to perform a job is accurately estimated. On the basis of this estimate the required number of employees is determined, suitable wage incentive schemes are devices and actual labour costs are worked out. The procedure followed in time study is to split the job into a number of component parts the time taken to perform each part of the job is ascertained and standard timings for different parts of a job are determined.

(2) Scientific selection, placement and training

To build up a team of efficient workers, Taylor realized that using scientific methods, instead of relying on intuition and judgement of the foremen should make selection. It implies selection of workers for the job by tallying job requirements with abilities and skills. Workers should be given placement on the basis of capability and aptitude. And, for developing the existing level of knowledge and potential scientific training should be imparted to workers on a regular basis.

(3) Standardization

By minutely studying metal-cutting operations, Taylor suggested that the scheme of standardization should be adopted in respect of trade tools and equipments, raw material used by workers and physical working conditions provided to them. Any difference in the quality of raw material, tools and equipments may directly affect level of efficiency of workers.

(4) Division of responsibility between management and workers

Taylor advocated that two aspects of planning, thinking and doing should be separated. Planning of work that is thinking process should be a responsibility of managers. They should design work standards by conducting various studies, devise incentive scheme for workers, discipline them and assign work to them. Whereas role of workers should be confined to implementation of these plans. In this way benefits of division of labour and specialization may be secured.

(5) Functional foremanship

Taylor introduced and practiced the concept of functional foremanship. According to this concept instead of having one foreman as an in-charge for production department. All activities should be grouped into two groups namely planning forum and workshop forum. Each forum should have four supervisors to command over the activities of workers. In doing so dual command emerges, because each worker will get orders and instructions from eight supervisors dealing with different aspect of his job.

(6) Mental revolution

In order to get desired results of scientific management there should be complete mental revolution on the part of workers as well as management. Mental revolution is a process of bringing drastic changes in their attitude, outlook and behavioural pattern in respect of their duties toward work, toward their fellow workers and employers. Similar kind of changes in outlook should also take place among managers towards workers and their problems. To bring the change in the mental attitude of both sides, Taylor suggested scheme of workers participation in management and sharing surplus as bonus.

(7) Differential payment

F.W.Taylor firmly believed that man is motivated by economic considerations. He, therefore, introduced a new payment plan called 'the differential piece work'. He linked incentives with production. Accordingly a worker will be paid in direct proportion to how much be produced. That is a worker will receive low piece rate if he produces the standard number of pieces and high rates if he surpasses the standard. In the latter case, the higher rate would be applied to all the pieces the worker produced, including those which were produced according to the standard.

1.10.1.2 Administrative Theory of Management

Though administrative theory of management is based on the contributions of many scholars and practitioners like Henri Fayol, Max Weber, Sheldon, Mooney, Allen and Urwick, etc. But major part of it relates to Foyal's work.

Henry Fayol's Administrative Theory of Management

Henri Fayol (1841-1925) is considered the ***'Father of administrative management theory'*** with focus on the development of broad administrative principles applicable to general and higher managerial levels. Foyal started his career as a junior engineer in a coal mining company in France in 1860 and became its general manager in 1880. He wrote a monograph in French in 1916, entitled "General and Industrial Administration" which was translated into English in 1929.

It is in four parts of which the first part deals with classification of business activities as technical activities (manufacturing or production), commercial activities (buying, selling and exchange), financial activities (raising and optimum use of capital), accounting activities (recording, costing and statistics), security activities (protection of persons and property), and administrative or managerial activities.

Second part contained basic functions of management performed by the managers in all types of organizations. In this way he identified five elements or functions of management process: Planning, organizing, commanding, coordinating and controlling.

Third part consists of 14 principles of management as general guides to the management process and management practice. These are as under.

(1) Division of Work. Division of work in the management process produces more and better work with the same effort. Various functions of management like planning, organizing, directing and controlling cannot be performed efficiently by a single proprietor or by a group of directors. They must be entrusted to specialists in related fields.

(2) Authority and Responsibility. As the management consists of getting the work done through others, it implies that the manager should have the right to give orders and power to exact obedience. A manager may exercise formal authority and also personal power. Formal authority is derived from his official position, while personal power is the result of intelligence, experience, moral worth, ability to lead, past service, etc. Responsibility is closely related to authority and it arises wherever authority is exercised. An individual, who is willing to exercise authority, must also be prepared to bear responsibility to perform the work in the manner desired. However, responsibility is feared as much as authority is sought after.

(3) Discipline. Discipline is absolutely essential for the smooth running of business. By discipline we mean, the obedience to authority, observance of the rules of service and norms of performance, respect for agreements, sincere efforts for completing the given job, respect for superiors, etc.

(4) Unit of Command. This principle requires that each employee should receive instructions about a particular work from one superior only. Foyal believed that if an employee was to report to more than one superior, he would be confused due to conflict in instructions and also it would be difficult to pinpoint responsibility to him.

(5) Unity of Direction. It means that there should be complete identity between individual and organizational goals on the one hand and between departmental goals inter se on the other. They should not pull in different directions.

(6) Subordination of Individual Interest to General Interest. In a business concern, an individual is always interested in maximizing his own satisfaction through more money, recognition, status, etc. This is very often against the general interest, which lies in maximizing production. Hence the need to subordinate the individual interest to general interest.

(7) Remuneration. The remuneration paid to the personnel of the firm should be fair. It should be based on general business conditions, cost of living, and productivity of the concerned employees and the capacity of the firm to pay. Fair remuneration increases workers' efficiency and morale and fosters good relations between them and the management.

(8) Centralization. If subordinates are given more role and importance in the management and organization of the firm, it is decentralization but if they are given less role and importance, it is centralization. The management must decide the degree of centralization or decentralization of authority on the basis of the nature of the circumstances, size of the undertaking, and the type of activities and the nature of organizational structure. The objective to pursue should be the optimum utilization of all faculties of the personnel.

(9) Scalar Chain. Scalar chain means the hierarchy of authority from the highest executive to the lowest one for the purpose of communication. It states superior subordinate relationship and the authority of superiors in relation to subordinate at various levels. As per this principle, the orders or communications should pass through the proper channels of authority along the scalar chain. But in case there is need for swift action, the proper channels of authority may be short-circuited by making direct contact (called gang plank) with the concerned authority.

(10) Order. To put things in an order needs effort. Disorder does not need any effort. It evolves by itself. Management should obtain orderliness in work through suitable organization of men and materials. The management should observe the principles of "right place for everything and for every man".

(11) Equity. Equity means equality of fair treatment. Equity results from a combination of kindness and justice. Employees expect management to be equally just to everybody. It requires managers to be free from all prejudices, personal likes or dislikes. Equity ensures healthy industrial relations between management and labour which is essential for the successful working of the enterprise.

(12) Stability of Tenure of Personnel. In order to motivate workers to do more and better work, it is necessary that they should be assured security of job by the management. If they have fear of insecurity of job, their morale will be low and they cannot give more and better work. Further, they will not have any sense of attachment to the firm and they will always be on the lookout for a job elsewhere.

(13) Initiative. Initiative means freedom to think out and execute a plan. The zeal and energy of employees are augmented by initiative. Innovation, which is the hallmark of technological progress, is possible only where the employees are encouraged to take initiative. According to Fayol, initiative is one of the keenest satisfactions for an intelligent man to experience, and hence, he advises managers to give their employees sufficient scope to show their initiative. Employees should be encouraged to make all kinds of suggestions to conceive and carry out their plans, even when some mistakes result.

(14) Esprit De-Corps. This means team spirit. Since "Union is strength", the management should create team spirit among the employees. Only when all the personnel pull together as a team, there is scope for realizing the objectives of the concern. Harmony and unity among the staff are a great source of strength to the undertaking. To achieve this, Fayol suggested two things. One, the motto of divide and rule should be avoided, and two, verbal communication should be used for removing misunderstandings.

Fourth part of monograph deals with managerial qualities and skills, which should be possessed by the managers. These are as: Physical qualities (health, vigour, personality), Mental ability (abilities to understand and learn, to make decisions and creativity, etc.), Moral education (Loyalty, dignity, ethical values, etc.), General education, Special knowledge and experience (knowledge arising out of practice).

1.10. 2. Behavioural or Neo-classical Approach

Behavioural approach was evolved gradually over many years. This is based on strong conviction that successful management depends on the ability of managers to understand the work, and background, needs, values, perceptions and personality of people. ***This approach will be studied on the following two phases, namely, Human Relation movement and Behavioural science approach.***

(*a*) **Human Relation Movement.** Under this approach Elton Mayo, Mary Parker, Follet, and Douglas McGregor have been the main contributors to this approach. Among the above contributors Elton Mayo's Hawthorne studies is very popular.

(*b*) **Behavioural Science Approach.** In view of certain inadequacies and drawbacks associated with human relation approach, many other social and behavioural scientists for undertaking and analyzing human behaviour methodically made concerted efforts. The term behavioural approach may be defined as systematic and scientific analysis of human behaviour with a view to determine causes of working behaviour of an individual. ***This approach is also known as "Organizational behaviour Approach".*** It includes an interdisciplinary approach of studying human behaviour consisting of psychology, sociology, physical and biological and cultural variables of individuals. For this approach, different views were developed by various behavioural scientists such as Douglas, McGregor, Abraham Maslow, Chester Bernard, Renis Likert and Herbert Simon.

1.10. 3. Modern Approach to Management

Modern approach represents latest developments, which took place after 1950. ***This approach can be studied in the following four phases namely, Quantitative approach, System approach, Contingent approach and Attributes of excellence.***

1.10.3.1. Quantitative Approach

This approach also known as 'management science approach', has been developed during 1950. It is based on the approach of scientific management. It offers systematic and scientific analysis and solution to the problems faced by managers. The quantitative approach aims at achieving high degree of precision, perfection and objectivity by encouraging the use of mathematical and statistical tools for solving complex problems. These quantitative decision making tools are known as 'Operations Research' like LPP, Simulation, queuing theory and game theory etc. It also implies use of computer-aided technology in various fields like production, finance, costing, transporting and storage etc. In simple terms, operations research may be regarded as application of scientific methods for solving problems and scientific methods consist of the following stages.

- Dividing problems into small and simple components
- Gathering required information on each component
- Analysis of data so collected
- Finding out solution to problem in hand.

The quantitative approach which involves use of knowledge and skills of several other disciplines such as statistics, engineering and accounting etc. has contributed significantly to management theory and behaviour. This approach has very limited application that too only in respect of problem solving and decision-making.

1.10.3.2. Systems Approach

Systems approach of management represents new thinking and latest developments related to organization and management. It was developed after 1950 emphasing interdependence and interrelationship among various activities of organization. Basically this approach aims at identifying the nature of relationship among various components of the organization, which is considered as larger system. The term system may be defined as a set of interrelated and interacting components assembled in a particular sequence as to produce some results. These components may also viewed as sub-systems of larger system. It is only through this sub-systems the larger system operates, thus larger system can be viewed as a whole entity or totality. The various sub-systems which are involved in the functioning of larger one are closely related to each other and to a system as a whole. Similarly, these sub-systems interact with each other by getting influenced and influencing others. Every system has sub-system and every sub-system may be considered as a system because, it may have a sub-systems.

The system approach defines an organization as a complex whole consisting of mutually interdependent and interacting parts, which are viewed as sub-system. Therefore the approach is said to be holistic in nature assuming that whole is greater than the sum of its parts.

The system may be broadly classified into four categories. They are as follows

- Physical system
- Mechanical system
- Biological system
- Social systems.

Physical systems are the part and parcel of the nature or sub-system, of it totally governed and regulated by the nature. For example, solar system, seasons and rivers, etc.

Mechanical systems refer to those devices, which are based on technology. These systems have been innovated by human beings for their betterment but are totally closed systems in nature, as they do not interact with external environment such as machines, motorcars, electronic appliances and consumer durables etc...

Biological systems are those systems, which regulate and control existence and survival of all living species, human and plants are good examples of biological systems.

Social systems may be defined as systems, which have been developed by human being to facilitate co-operative working to overcome the problem of isolation and desolation. All kinds of small and big formal and informal and economic and non economic organizations are examples of social systems.

1.10.3.3. Contingency Approach

Contingency approach, though related to system approach, represents comparatively new line of thinking among management scientists. This approach basically aims at attempting to take a step away from universal application of managerial principles a recommending that the application of these principles is subject to appropriateness of the situation. It is a systematic attempt to determine package of management technique, approaches and practices which are appropriate in specific situation.

The contingency approach offers following guidelines for the managers.

- Contingency approach is situation oriented urging upon the managers to study, analyse and diagnose the situation. It is to be done in terms of components variables of the situation and external factors affecting the situation.
- Subsequently, after the analysis of the situation, the managers are expected to prepare inventories of management theory, principle, techniques and concepts.
- In order to tackle the situation efficiently the validity and applicability of management tools and techniques is to be examined and finally package of these tools and techniques is prepared which is appropriate for that specific situation. The different situation requires different managerial response.

1.11. DIFFERENCE BETWEEN MANAGEMENT AND ADMINISTRATION

Sl.No	Point of Distinction	Administration	Management
1	Definition	Administration means overall determination of policies, settings of major objectives, the laying out of broad programmes, major projects and so forth.(ie., Administration means determination of goals, formulation of plans and policies of the organization.)	Management means essentially an executive function, the active direction of human efforts getting things done.(i.e., Management is considered as an operative function of carrying out plans and policies for achieving objectives.)
2	Nature	Deterministic or thinking function	Executive or doing function
3	Scope	It is concerned with the determination of major objectives and policies	It is concerned with the implementation of policies
4	Level	It is mainly a top-level function	It is largely a middle and lower-level function
5	Influence	Administrative decisions are influenced mainly by public opinion and other outside forces.	Managerial decisions are influenced mainly by objectives and policies of the organization
6	Direction of human efforts	It is not directly concerned with the direction of human efforts	It is actively concerned with the direction of human efforts in the execution of plans
7	Main function	Planning and control are the main functions involved in it	Directing and organizing are the main functions involved in it.
8	Skills required	Conceptual & human skills	Technical and human skills
9	Usage	Used largely in government and public sector	Used mainly in business organizations
10	Examples	Minister, Commander, Commissioner, Registrar, vice-Chancellor, Governor etc.	Managing Director, General Manager, Sales Manager, Branch Manager etc.

1.12. MANAGEMENT AS A SCIENCE OR AN ART

1.12.1. Management as a Science

Science is not only using the test tube or the lab coat, but also they are implicit in the method of inquiry used by a discipline for gathering data. We can call it as a discipline, as it is a scientific on the following grounds:

1. Methods of inquiry are systematic and empirical;
2. Information can be gathered, recorded and analysed; and
3. Results are cumulative and communicable.

Systematic means the recorded and analyzed data or being ordered and unbiased. All scientific information collected as raw data and finally ordered and analysed with the help of statistical tools. It thus becomes communicable and intellectual. Communication of results also permits repetition of the study, if need, by the investigator or others. When the study is repeated and the second try provides results similar to the first one, which derives much more confidence in those results.

On the basis of the above definition of science we may perceive the management is also a science. ***The word 'science' is used to denote two types of systematic knowledge: natural or exact and behavioural or inexact.*** Some more explanation of the scientific nature of management is needed. Management is not like the exact or natural sciences such as physics, chemistry, etc. Management is a behavioural/social science. It is possible for us to study the effects of any one of the factors affecting a phenomenon individually by making the other factors in operative for the time being. For example, in physics it is possible for anyone to study in a laboratory, the effects of, say, only heat on the density of air by holding other factors (such as humidity, etc) constant for the duration of the experiment. But the same thing is not possible in management where we have to study man and a multiplicity of factors affecting him. It is not possible to study the effect of, say, only monetary incentives on a worker's productivity because this effect will always be found to be mixed with and inseparable from other factors such as the leadership style of the worker's supervisor, worker's need hierarchy, the pressure of his co-workers, etc. At best, we can get only a rough idea of the relationship between the two. In other words, our findings are not going to be as accurate and dependable as those of the physical sciences. We may tell about tendencies and probabilities of management. We may, therefore, place management in the category of a behavioural science.

1.12.2. Management as an Art

Art is concerned with the understanding of how a particular work can be accomplished. Management in this sense is an art. It is the art of getting things done through others in dynamic and mostly non-repetitive situations. Whether it is a factory or a firm the resources like men, machine and money have to be coordinated against several constraints to achieve given objectives in the most efficient manner. The manager has to constantly analyse the existing situation, determine the objectives, seek alternatives, implement, coordinate, control and evaluate information and make decisions.

Knowledge of management theory and principles is indeed a valuable aid and kit of the manager but it cannot replace his other managerial skills and qualities. This knowledge has to be applied and practiced by the manager just as the medical or legal practitioners practice their respective sciences. In this sense, management is an art. It is like the art of a musician or the art of a painter who seeks to achieve the desired effect with colour or instruments, but mainly with his own skill.

We may thus conclude that management involves both elements those of a science and an art. While certain aspects of management make it a science, certain others, which involve application of skill, make it an art.

1.13. DIFFERENCE BETWEEN MANAGERS AND ENTREPRENEURS

An Entrepreneur

An entrepreneur is the person (or group of persons) at the top of any business concern who undertake financial and legal responsibility for the success or failure of the concern.

Decision-making by the entrepreneur is mainly with regard to the following

- Goals and objectives of the enterprise and broadly how these are to be accomplished.
- The kind of image the enterprise is to project of itself and how it is to conduct it self in general.
- The kind of products to be manufactured whether top quality and useful products, or low quality and not so useful products.
- The concern's attitude towards its employees, the government, society and so on.

Manager

A manager is an employee of the entrepreneur. His job is to work for the accomplishment of the goals and objectives set by the entrepreneur.

There may be cases where a person is both an entrepreneur and a manager at the same time as, for example, in the case of the sole proprietor or the managing partner of a firm. Even so the managerial functions performed by him in this capacity are the same as those of any non-owner manager.

Difference between Entrepreneur and Manager

The main difference between an entrepreneur and a manager is with regard to the degree of freedom enjoyed in his work. Being the owner of the undertaking, the entrepreneur is free to determine the objectives based on his own assessment, beliefs and values. Limitations imposed by the external environment and, to a certain extent, availability of resources will also influence him in this regard. However, the manager is only concerned with the direction and coordination of the resources to accomplish the objectives in the determination of which he may, or may not have had any role. In any case, his own values and beliefs have necessarily to take a back seat because the nature of his work requires him to act rationally and thoughtfully toward the accomplishment of organizational objectives.

1.14. DISTINGUISH BETWEEN THE MANAGER AND THE LEADER

Manager	Leader
He drives and orders	He coaches and advises
He depends on his authority	He depends on his confidence and goodwill
He engenders fear	He inspires enthusiasm
He fixes blames and finds faults	He solves problems
He knows all the answers	He consults and seeks advice
He makes the work drudgery	He makes the work, a game
He believes in "I"	He believes in "We" and "Your"

1.14.1 Business Environment

Business environment is classified into micro environment and macro environment.

(*a*) **Micro environment.** Micro environment consists of the elements of suppliers, customers. intermediaries, competitors and the general public. These are considered as controllable factors.

(*b*) **Macro environment.** The term "Macro environment" consists of demographic, economic, political legal, socio-cultural, physical and technological forces which are uncontrollable. These are all uncontrollable as far as the business is concerned.

Now we shall discuss the impact of these environment forces.

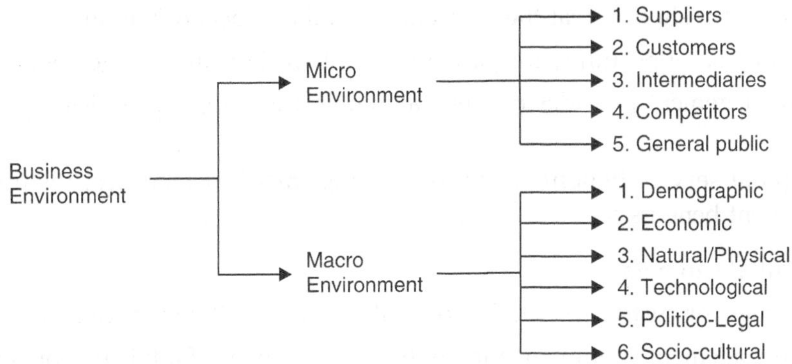

1.14.2 Social Responsibilities

Meaning

The term 'social responsibility' is related with public interest and social welfare. Society is the part of the management to initiate actions either to protect social interest of the society.

Definition

According to Keith Davis, the term Social responsibility refers to two types of business obligations, viz. (*a*) the socio-economic obligation, and (*b*) the socio-human obligation.

The socio-economic obligation of every business is to see that the economic consequences of its actions do not adversely affect public welfare. This includes obligations to promote employment opportunities, to maintain competition, to curb inflation etc.

The socio-human obligation of every business is to nurture and develop human values such as morale, cooperation, motivation and self-realization in work.

Social Responsibility of Management towards different groups

Social responsibility requires management to identify the various interest groups, which affect its functioning, and which are also affected by its functioning. These interest groups are shareholder, employees, customers, surplus, society and government.

Responsibility to Shareholders

- The management has a responsibility to provide safeguard to the money invested by shareholders.

- The management protects the interest of the majority shareholders and large minority of shareholders.
- The management provides to the shareholder a reasonable dividend and
- The management should report the day to day activities and strengths and weaknesses of the organization to the shareholders.

Responsibility to Employees

- The management should pay fair and reasonable remuneration for their work
- The management to make the work place rather safe and pleasant
- Management should treat the workers as another wheel of the cart
- Providing an opportunity for participation of workers in management
- The management provides proper training and develops the efficiency of the workers and
- Adequate service benefits such as housing, medical facilities, insurance coverage retirement benefits.

Responsibility of Customers

- Consumers or customers satisfaction is the aim of all the management
- The management should encourage the establishment of advisory council
- The management should not indulge in profiteering, boarding, scarcity
- The distribution of goods should easily reach the customers
- The management should not mislead the customers by false, misleading and exaggerated advertisements
- Regular supplies of right quality goods at right time and right place
- Charge reasonable prices
- Prompt, adequate and continuous services
- Charge reasonable prices
- Prompt, adequate and continuous services
- Prompt, redressal of customer's grievances and
- True and fair information through advertisements.

Responsibility to Suppliers

- The management should provide correct information regarding its financial position to its suppliers and creditors
- The management should create healthy relationship to the suppliers and
- The management should make prompt payment.

Responsibility to Society

- To provide maximum possible or efficient use of the society's resources
- To provide maximum possible employment opportunities

- To keep the environment healthy and free from all types of pollution
- To contribute to the upliftment of the weaker sections of society
- To refrain from indulging in anti-social and unethical practices and
- To improve public health, education and cultural life of the community.

Responsibility to Government

- To abide by the laws of the country
- To pay taxes honestly and in time
- To avoid corrupting public servants
- To encourage fair trade practices and
- To avoid monopoly and concentration of economic power.

1.14.3 Social Audit

Meaning

Social audit is to measure the effectiveness of organization's social performance. It involves a commitment to systematic assessment of the company's main activities that have a social impact, and reporting to the society on relevant issues. It encompasses every possible area, such as pollution control, T & D, promotion of minorities and so on.

Definition

"A commitment to systematic assessment of and reporting on some meaningful, definable domain of the company's activities that have social impact."

—Raymond A.Bauer & Dan. H.Fenn

1.14.4 Management Ethics

Ethics

All individuals in business or non-business activities are concerned with some standardized form of behaviour is known as ethics.

Definition of Ethics

"The discipline dealing with what is good and bad and with moral duty and obligation."

—Webster's Dictionary

In the words of Garrett, "Business ethics is a study of moral rightness and wrongness of the acts involved in production, distribution and exchange of economic goods and services".

Ethics refer to value oriented decision and behaviour. The word ethics comes from Greek and mean char guiding beliefs, standards etc.

According to Thomas J.Adams, "Business ethics deals with the values of what is right and wrong, good and bad, and moral and immoral in business relationships."

Classification of Ethics

Ethics is classified into three categories. They are

(*a*) Personal ethics

(*b*) Accounting ethics

(*c*) Business ethics

(*a*) **Personal Ethics.** It referred to as "The rules by which an individual lives his/her personal life".

(*b*) **Accounting Ethics.** It constitutes the code* of conduct for the accounting professionals.

(*c*) **Business Ethics.** It is concerned with truth and justice in conducting business affairs. It encompasses a variety of aspects such as expectations of society, fair competition, advertising, public relation, social responsibilities, consumer autonomy and corporate behaviour in the home country as well as abroad. To charge fair from the customers to pay tax in the Govt.

Types of Ethical Theories

There are three types of ethical theories viz., **Utilization theory, Right based theory,** and **Theory of justice.**

Utilization theory

It suggests that plans and actions should be evaluated by their consequences. The underlying idea is that plans or actions should produce the greatest good for the greatest number of people.

Right based theory

It holds that all people have basic rights. A number of rights can be found in the constitution. For example, the rights to freedom of conscience free speech and due process.

Theory of Justice

It demands that fairness and equity as well as impartiality guide decision-makers.

* **Code: It is a statement of policies, principles, or rules that guide behaviour.**

Characteristics of Ethics in Management

- Ethics may be thought of in terms of a mass of moral principles.
- It is concerned with truth and justice and has a variety of aspects such as expectation of society, fair competition, advertising and public relations.
- Ethics deals with what is good and bad, moral duty and obligation.
- Ethics as an art it involves techniques of judging and decision making as well as the tools of social control and personal development.

Importance for Management Ethics

- Increases business ethics survival of the business unit is not difficult.
- The customers and public always honor an ethically practicing company.
- Ethical management improves better decision-making ability all the business activities.
- A businessman observes ethics strictly, definitely the particular business unit well developed.

- Ethical attitude management improves the confidence of the customers, employees and society.
- Ethical attitude improves the coordination of the employees.

Factors affecting Business Ethics

1. Political uncertainty leads to affect business ethics.
2. Corruption enters the government offices.
3. Businessman must know the ethics but he does not know affect the business ethics.
4. Non-cooperation of workers leads to immoral business activities.
5. The trade union has break business ethics.
6. Superiors in the organization doing immoral activities leads to unethical to their subordinates in the organization.
7. The ethical climate of country is poor ethics in the inside of the organization also poor.

Factors that raise ethical standards [or] implementation of Ethics in Management

- Appointment of ethics committee consisting of internal and external directors.
- Conduct regular meetings to discuss ethical issues.
- Communicating the code to all members of the organization.
- Good behaviour is rewarded and bad behaviour is punished.
- The committee follows up and updating the code is important process.
- Submit the report to the board of directors the activities of committee.

Benefits of Management Ethics

- **Customers**
  - Quality product.
  - Reasonable price
  - Good Service
  - No price discrimination
- **Employees**
  - Fair wages
  - Job security
  - Participation of management
  - Better working condition
  - Better moralities.
- **Business**
  - Increase the profit
  - Get good will
  - Less labour turnover
- **Government**
  - Development of national economy
  - Prompt collection of taxes.

Chapter 2 PLANNING

2.1. MEANING

Planning is the fundamental/primary function of management. Planning is the function that determines in advance what should be done. It is looking ahead and preparing for the future. It is a process of deciding the business objectives and charting out the methods of attaining those objectives. In other words, it is the determination of what is to be done, how and where it is to be done, who is to do it and how results are to be evaluated. Plans made by top management of the organizations whole may cover periods as long as five or ten years. Also, plans made by middle or first line managers, cover such shorter periods. Such plans may be for the next days or weeks, or months, etc... for example, for a two-hour meeting to take place in a week.

2.2. DEFINITION OF PLANNING

There are numerous definitions of planning. Different experts have defined different points of view.

> *"Planning is an intellectual process, the conscious determination of course of action, the basing of decision on purpose, acts and considered estimates".* —*Koontz & O'Donnell*

> *"Planning is deciding in advance what is to be done. When a manager plans, he projects a course of action, for the future, attempting to achieve a consistent, coordinated structure of operations aimed at the desired results".* —*Theo Haimann*

> *"Planning is the thinking process, the organized foresight, the vision based on fact and experience that is required for intelligent action".* —*Alford & Beatty*

2.3. NATURE OF PLANNING (CHARACTERISTICS/FEATURES OF PLANNING)

1. Planning is goal-oriented. Planning involves setting the objectives of an organization for achieving the business targets well in time. Objectives can easily be achieved by a sound planning process.

2. Planning is a primacy. Planning precedes other functions in the management process. It is the primary requisite before other managerial functions step in. The other managerial functions, viz., organizing, staffing, directing & controlling can be performed only after the necessary planning has been done. So it gets primary everywhere.

3. Planning is all-pervasive. Planning is a pervasive activity covering the entire enterprise with all its segments and every levels of management. It is equally important for large and small firms.

4. Planning is an intellectual/rational process. Planning is a mental exercise involving imagination, foresight and sound judgement. It is not guesswork or wishful thinking. Managers take the necessary steps to fight against future events. So it is a process of looking ahead.

5. Planning is a continuous process. Planning is a never-ending activity. It is a dynamic exercise. One plan makes another plan to be followed by a series of other plans. Again constant changes make planning a continuous activity.

6. Planning is a precision. The meaning, scope and nature of planning must be precise. It must pinpoint the expected results exactly. Any error in planning may lead to serious mistakes in the other functions.

7. Planning involves choice. Planning is essentially decision-making or choosing among alternative courses of action. Planning presupposes the existence of alternatives. Plans are decisions made after evaluation of alternative courses of action. A planning problem arises only when an alternative course of action is discovered.

8. Planning is directed towards efficiency. In general, all management functions including planning is directed towards increase the efficiency of the firm. Corollary of planning is (*a*) Planning is an intellectual activity that aims the best way of doing things, and (*b*) planning provides with goals and objectives. Thus planning is directed towards efficiency.

9. Flexibility of planning. Planning is flexible as commitment, which is based on future course of action. These are always dynamic. Therefore, an adjustment is needed between the various factors and planning.

2.4. IMPORTANCE OF PLANNING

(*a*) **Minimizes Risk and Uncertainty.** In today's increasingly complex organizations, intuition alone can no longer be relied upon as a means for making decisions. This is one reason why planning has become so important. By providing a more rational, fact-based procedure for making decisions, planning allows managers and organisations to minimise risk and uncertainty. In a dynamic society such as ours, in which social and economic conditions alter rapidly, planning helps the manager to cope with and prepare for the changing environment. Planning does not deal with future decisions, but with the futurity of present decisions. The manager has a feeling of being in control if he has anticipated some of the possible changes and has planned for them. It is like going out with an umbrella in cloudy weather. It is through planning that the manager relates the uncertainties and possibilities of tomorrow to the facts of today and yesterday.

(*b*) **Leads to Success.** Planning does not guarantee success, but studies have shown that, often things being equal, companies which plan not only outperform the non planners but also outperform their own past results. This may be because when a businessman's actions are not random or ad hoc, arising as mere reaction to the market place, i.e., when his actions are planned, be definitely does better. Military historians attribute much of the success of the world's greatest generals to effective battle plans.

Planning leads to success by going beyond mere adaptation to market fluctuations. It proacts. It involves an attempt to shape the environment on the belief that business is not just the creation of environment but its creator as well.

(*c*) **Focuses Attention on the Organization's Goals.** Planning helps the manager to focus attention on the organisation's goals and activities. This makes it easier to apply and coordinate the resources of the organisation more efficiently. The whole organisation is forced to embrace identical goals and collaborate in achieving them. It also enables the manager to chalkout in advance an orderly sequence of steps for the realisation of an organisation's goals and to avoid a needless overlapping of activities.

(*d*) **Facilitates Control.** In planning, the manager sets goals and develops plans to accomplish these goals. These goals and plans then become standards or benchmarks against which performance can be measured. The function of control is to ensure the activities conform to the plans. Thus, controls can be exercised only if there are plans.

2.5. STEPS IN PLANNING/PLANNING PROCESS

The steps generally involved in planning are as follows:

- *Establishing Verifiable Goals or Set of Goals to be achieved*
- *Establishing Planning Premises*
- *Deciding the Planning Period*
- *Finding Alternative Courses of Action*
- *Evaluating and Selecting a Course of Action*
- *Developing Derivative Plans*
- *Measuring and Controlling the Progress*

1. Establishing Verifiable Goals or Set of Goals to be Achieved. The first step in planning is to determine the enterprise objectives. Upper level or top-level managers most often set these, usually after a number of possible objectives have been carefully considered. ***There are many types of objectives managers may select such as a desired sales volume or growth rate, the development of a new product or service, or even a more abstract goal such as becoming more active in the***

community. The type of goal selected will depend on a number of factors like the basic mission of the organization, the values its managers hold, and the actual and potential abilities of the organization.

2. Establishing Planning Premises. The second step in planning is to establish planning premises. ***Plans are prepared for future. But future is uncertain. Therefore, management makes certain assumptions about the future. These assumptions are known as planning premises.*** Planning premises are vital to the success of planning as they supply pertinent facts and information relating to the future such as population trends, the general economic conditions, production costs and prices, probable competitive behaviour, capital and material availability, governmental control and so on.

Planning premises can be variously classified as under:

- ***Internal and external premises.***
- ***Tangible and intangible premises.***
- ***Controllable and non-controllable premises.***

(a) ***Internal and external premises. Internal Premises refer to the factors within the enterprise.*** These include sales forecasts, policies and programs of the organization, capital investment in plant and equipment, skill of the labour force, other resources and abilities of the organization in the form of machines, money and methods, and beliefs, behaviour and values of the owners and employees of the organization.

External premises are those, which lie outside of the firm. It may be classified in three group's viz.,

(i) General business environment including economic, political and social conditions,

(ii) The product market consisting of the demand and supply forces for the product or services, and

(iii) Factors, which affect the resources available to the enterprise.

(b) ***Tangible and intangible premises.*** Some of the planning premises may be tangible while some others may be intangible. Tangible premises are those, which can be quantitatively measured. For example, population growth, industry demand, capital and resources invested in the organization are all tangible premises whose quantitative measurement is possible.

Intangible premises are which being qualitative in character cannot be so measured. For example, political stability, sociological factors, business and economic environment, attitudes, philosophies and behaviour of the owners of the organization are all intangible premises whose quantitative measurement is not possible.

(c) ***Controllable and non-controllable premises.*** Those while some of the planning premises may be controllable, some others are non-controllable. Those premises, which are entirely within the control and realm of management, are known as controllable premises. Some of the examples of controllable factors are the company's advertising policy, competence of management members, skill of the labour force, availability of resources in terms of capital and labour, attitude and behaviour of the owners of the organization etc.

Premises over which an enterprise has absolutely no control are uncontrollable premises. Some of the examples of uncontrollable factors are strikes, wars, natural calamities, emergency, legislation, etc.

3. Deciding the Planning Period. Once upper-level managers have selected the basic long-term goals and the planning premises, the next task is to decide the period of the plan. Businesses vary considerably in their planning periods. In some instances plans are made for a year only while in others they span decades. In each case, however, there is always some logic in selecting a particular time range for planning. Companies generally base their period on a future that can reasonably be anticipated. Other factors, which influence the choice of a period are as follows: (*a*) lead time in development and commercialization of a new product, (*b*) time required to recover capital investments or the pay-back period; and (*c*) length of commitments already made.

(*a*) ***Lead time in development and commercialization of a new product.*** For example, a heavy engineering company planning to start a new project should have a planning period of, say, five years with one or two years for conception, engineering and development and as many more years for production and sales. On the contrary, a small manufacturer of spare parts who can commercialize his idea in a year or so need make annual plans only.

(*b*) ***Time required to recovering capital investments or the payback period.*** These are the number of years over which the investment outlay will be recovered or paid back from the cash inflow if the estimates turn out to be correct. If a machine costs ₹ 10 lakhs and generates cash inflow of ₹ 2 lakhs a year, it has a pay-back period of five years. Therefore, the plan should also be for at least five years.

(*c*) ***Length of commitments already made.*** The plan period should, as far as possible, be long enough to enable the fulfillment of commitments already made. For example, if a company has agreed to supply goods to the buyers for five years or has agreed to work out mines for ten years it need also plan for the same period to fulfil its commitments. However, if the length of commitment can somehow be reduced, the plan period can also be reduced. Thus, if the company can grant sub-lease of its mines to other parties, then it can reduce its plan period also.

4. Finding Alternative Courses of Action. The fourth step in planning is to search for and examining alternative courses of action. Generally, there are alternative ways of achieving the same goals. For example, in order to increase sales, an enterprise may launch advertising campaign or reduce prices or increase the quality of products. Therefore, alternative course of action should be determined. This requires imagination, foresight and ingenuity. In determining alternatives the critical or limiting factors must be kept in view.

5. Evaluating and Selecting a Course of Action. Having sought alternative courses, the fifth step is to evaluate them in the light of the premises and goals and to select the best course or courses of action. Alternative courses of action can be evaluated against the criteria of cost, risks, benefit and organizational facilities. The strong and weak points of every alternative should be analyzed carefully. This is done with the help of quantitative techniques and operations research.

6. Developing Derivative Plans. Once the plan has been formulated, its broad goals must be translated into day-to-day operations of the organization. Middle and lower-level managers must draw up the appropriate plans, programmes and budgets for their sub-units. These are known as derivative *plans*. In developing these derivative plans, lower-level managers take steps similar to those taken by upper-level managers-selecting realistic goals, assessing their sub-units' particular strengths and weaknesses and analyzing those parts of the environment that can affect them.

7. Measuring and Controlling the Progress. Obviously, it is foolish to let a plan run its course without monitoring its progress. Hence the process of controlling is a critical part of any plan. Managers need to check the progress of their plans so that they can (a) take whatever remedial action is necessary to make the plan work, or (b) change the original plan if it is unrealistic.

2.6. TYPES OF PLANNING (HIERARCHY OF PLANNING)

From the viewpoint of scope and span of time, planning can be classified as under:

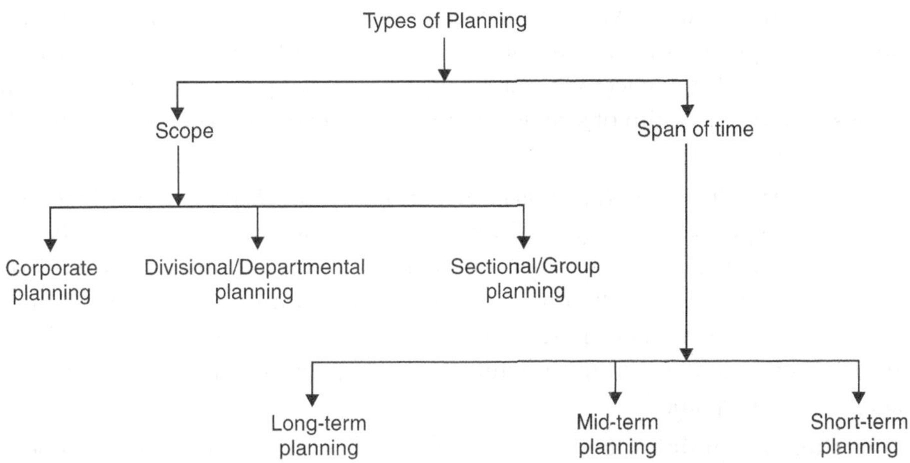

(*i*) **Corporate Planning.** ***Planning for the company as a whole is known as corporate planning.*** It lays down objectives, strategies and policies for the entire organization. The purpose of corporate planning is to determine the long-term goals of an enterprise and generate plans to achieve these goals keeping in view the probable changes in its environment. It is proactive planning as it provides for future contingencies. It is less detailed and specific than sectional and divisional planning. It is designed to steer successfully the enterprise through various contingencies. It is done at the top-level management. It is very broad and general. For example, increasing the company's market share by ten per cent in next five years, becoming a technological leader in industry, earning a 25% rate of return on investment and so on.

(*ii*) **Departmental or Divisional Planning.** It includes the plans formulated for various departments or divisions of an enterprise. It determines the scope and activities of a particular department. For example, sales budget, production budget, finance budget are departmental plans.

In a multi-product company there may be several product divisions, for example, sugar division, textile division, chemical division etc. each division formulates its overall plan by integrating all sectional plans relating to that division. For instance, sales plan is a synthesis of advertising, sales promotion, pricing, channel of distribution and product plans. Departmental plans are formulated at the middle level of management and approved by the top management. *These plans are also known as functional plans because every department or division is concerned with one particular major function of business.* Such planning is segmental and reactive in nature.

(*iii*) **Group or Sectional Planning.** Group or sectional planning refers to planning for specific groups or sections within a department or division. Such plans are prepared to implement departmental or divisional plans. For example, the advertising section may prepare a sectional plan-to execute the sales plan of the company. Similarly, the purchase section may prepare a purchase plan to attain the goals of the production department. Such planning is also known as Unit planning. The focus is on day-to-day work and on meeting schedules and targets. It is action-oriented. Sectional plans are formulated by operating level of management and it has to be approved by higher authorities.

(*iv*) **Long-range Planning.** ***It is also known as strategic planning.*** It covers a long period of time say 5,10 or more years in future. It takes into account the forecasted changes in the environment over the long-term. It provides the overall targets towards which all activities of the organization are to be directed. It results in long-term commitment of resources. It involves a great deal of uncertainty because the period involved is several years. It tries to match the resources of the organization (micro aspect) with the environmental threats and opportunities (macro aspect). A long-term strategic plan takes a macro view of the organization. It provides direction for the growth of the enterprise. The primary aim of strategic planning is to enable the enterprise to affect rather than accept the future.

(*v*) **Medium-term Planning.** ***It is also known as intermediate planning or tactical planning.*** Such planning covers a period between 1 to 5 years. It is more detailed and specific than long range strategic planning. It is designed to implement strategic plans by coordinating the work of different departments. Such planning is coordinative. A tactical plan is drawn up for short term moves and manoeuvres within the broader and more stable strategic plans. For example, a tactical plan may be drawn up to meet a sudden slump in demand, shortage of power etc. Tactical plans are less detailed than operational plans.

(*vi*) **Operational Planning.** Operational plans are prepared for a period up to one year. They are generally specific and detailed. These plans provide form and content to long-term plans. Such plans are prepared on the basis of strategic and tactical plans. The main purpose of operational planning is to maximize efficiency in day-to-day operations and ensure uniformity of action. For example, repairs and maintenance plan, purchase plan, product plan and so on.

Difference between Strategic and Tactical Planning

Strategic planning	Tactical planning
1. It decides the major goals and policies of allocation of resources to achieve these goals.	1. It decides the detailed use of resources for achieving each goal.
2. It is done at higher levels of management.	2. It is done at lower levels of management.
3. It is long-term.	3. It is short-term.
4. It is generally based on long-term forecasts about technology, political Environment, etc. and is more uncertain.	4. It is generally based on the past performance of the organization and is less uncertain.
5. It is less detailed because it is not involved with the day-to-day operations of the organisation.	5. It is more detailed because it is involved with the day-to-day operations of the organisation.

2.7. ESSENTIALS OF SOUND PLAN/MAKING AN EFFECTIVE PLANNING

A good plan should contain the following features

- It should be based on clearly defined objectives.
- It must be simple and easily understandable.
- It should be flexible or adaptable to changing conditions.
- It must be balanced in all respects and should be reasonably comprehensive.
- It should provide standards for the evaluation of performance and actions.
- It should be economical. i.e., permit optimum use of available resources before creating new authorities and new resources.
- It should be practicable or action oriented.
- It should be prepared with the consultation of concerned persons.
- Different plan must be properly integrated and harmonized with one another.
- It should provide for proper analysis and classification of actions.

2.8. TYPES OF PLANS

In a business enterprise, we find or hear of a number of plans; which might seem to be different in their contents and application. However, a careful analysis of various plans would reveal them to be closely connected and forming a sort of structure. Depending on their use, management plans may be classified into two broad categories.

Types of Plans

Standing Plan (or) Multi-use plan	**Single Use Plan (or) Ad hoc Plan**
Missions/purposes	*Programme*
Objectives/Goals	*Budgets*
Strategies	*Schedules*
Policies	*Projects*
Rules	*Methods*
Procedures	

I. Standing Plan

(*a*) **Mission or Purposes.** ***Mission is a statement that defines the role that an organization plays in the society.*** It represents the overall philosophy of an organization. It indicates the end which is to be achieved over the whole life of an organization or at least over a long period. The term mission is generally used in non-business organizations like a college, university, a religious trust, a club, a government etc. For example, the mission of the Government of India might be eradication of poverty; the mission of a university might be imparting higher level education to the largest possible number of people of society and encouraging research maximally; and the mission of a manufacturing enterprise might be producing high quality goods for the common men of society at the most affordable prices and so on.

(*b*) **Objectives or Goals.** ***Objectives are the results which management wants to achieve through the making and implementation of a plan***. These, in fact, are the goals towards which a plan is directed. Objectives provide a sense of direction to the thinking process of the planner, and to the action process of the operators of the plan. Organization objectives may be classified into two categories. They are Internal objectives and External objectives. An internal objective relates to maximize the company's profit, high liquidity, best services to employees, high return to shareholders etc. While external objectives relate to the services to the customers and their satisfaction. It is rightly pointed out that the management process begins with setting the organizational objectives. While establishing the organizational objectives, the following eight areas should be taken into account without fail

- Market standing
- Productivity
- Physical and financial resources
- Profitability
- Innovation
- Manager performance and development
- Work performance and attitude
- Public and social responsibility.

In addition to that the following two things also very essential for formulating objectives.

- The mission of the enterprise, and
- The resources and limitations of the enterprise.

In any case, objectives must be rational and must contribute to the mission of the enterprise.

(*c*) **Strategies.** ***It is a special type of plan prepared for meeting the challenges posed by the activities of competitors and other environmental forces***. It is an action to meet the specific demands of the situation. The concept of strategy is borrowed from military organizations. In the military plans are changed and modified very often for the purpose of meeting the movement of enemy. Similarly, the business enterprises, managers bring the changes in corporate plans and policies in accordance with the tactics adopted by competitors. The nature and form of strategy is not static, but it is a dynamic one.

(*d*) **Policies.** Since all managers in the organisation do planning from the highest to the lowest. It is imperative that planning by managers at lower levels must be within the limits of planning done at upper levels of management. For achieving this purpose precisely; policies are formulated by the top management.

A policy might be defined as ***"A statement of guidance and instruction; which defines and confines the area of discretion of subordinates, in matters of decision-making."***

For example, A policy of the marketing manager to extend credit to customers for a maximum period of 30 days; authorized salespersons to extend credit to their customers for any period say, a week, a fortnight, or 20 or 25 days; but in no case for a period beyond 30 days; which amounts to the boundary line of policy of credit to customers.

(*e*) **Rules.** ***A rule is a specific and detailed guide to action. It is also a standing plan, as they prescribe in advance what is to be done or not to be done in a specific situation. The top management derives rules.*** Rules must be strictly followed. Rules are definite and they do not leave any scope for discretion on the part of the subordinates. Rules for dealing with unauthorized absence from duty, "No smoking in the factory", and "Stop when the red light is on" are some examples of rules.

(*f*) **Procedures.** ***A procedure, as a type of management plan, specifies the manner of handling an organizational activity in terms of various steps to be undertaken,*** i.e., a procedure is a chronological sequence of steps to be undertaken to enforce a policy and to achieve an organizational objectives. The essence of a procedure is the chronological (i.e. in order of time) sequence of actions. For example, there might be specified procedures for handling inward mail; procedures for executing orders of customers; procedure for employees to proceed on to leave and so on, for various other organizational activities.

(II) Single Use plan

(*a*) **Programmes.** ***A programme is a plan of action indicating what work is to be done to carry out a particular objective.*** For example to popularize the products thereis a need for an advertising programme. Again, to improve the skills of personnel in performing their jobs; there is required a 'training and development' programme. For undertaking the manufacturing activities, there is a production programme, and so on.

(*b*) **Budgets.** ***A budget is a plan, which states expected results of a given future period in numerical terms. It is a plan of action or blueprint designed to achieve a specific goal. It may be expressed in time, money, or other measurable units.*** It is a projection defining the anticipated costs and results and the allocation of resources. It may reflect capital outlay, cash flow, production and sales targets. It expresses organizational objectives in financial and physical units. For example, man-hours, machine-hours, sales-targets, expense estimates in money terms or revenue estimates in money terms etc.

There are various types of budgets according to their nature. These are

- *Variable Budgets or Flexible Budget*

  These budgets vary according to the organization output.

- *Programme Budget*

  In this budget, the agency identifies goals, develops detailed programmes to meet the goals, and estimates the cost of each programme.

- *Zero-base Budget*

  It is a combination of programme and variable budget.

(*c*) **Schedules.** ***A schedule is a time-table of work. It specifies the date when a task is to begin and the time needed to complete each task.*** *The starting and completion date for each part of the programme are specified in the time schedule.*

Three main elements are involved in planning a schedule.

- *Identify activities or tasks,*
- *Determine their sequence, and*
- *Specify starting and finishing date for each activity as well as for the sequence as a whole.*

(*d*) **Projects.** ***A project is a complex scheme for the investment of resources, which can be analyzed and evaluated as an independent unit.*** The main features of a project are as follows.

- *It is a non-recurring plan.*
- *It has a specific mission or objective.*
- *It involves time bound plan with a long time.*
- *It has a clear termination point.*

(*e*) **Methods.** ***Methods specify the detailed and best manner to perform a particular step, comprised in a procedure.*** Methods are formalized and standardized ways of accomplishing repetitive and routine jobs. They are designed to keep operations running on planned and desired lines, to prevent confusion and adhocism and to ensure economy and efficiency. Methods provide detailed and specific guidance for day-to-day operations. Methods are helpful in the simplification, standardization and systematization of work. They serve as uniform norms to guide and control operations and performance. Standard methods represent the best way of performing jobs.

Summary of Various Plans

Name of Plan	Definition	Nature	Example
Objective	Goal or target to be achieved	Basis of all plans	Increase sales by 10 per cent
Policy	General statement or understanding to guide thinking	Boundary within which decisions are to be made	Employees are to be promoted on the basis of seniority
Strategy	Action plan to face environmental uncertainties	Relates the organisation to its environment	Combative advertising to face price cuts by competitors
Procedure	Manner in which activities are to be performed	Sequence of steps	Purchase procedure
Rule	States what should or should not be done in a given situation	Rigid plan, no scope for discretion	No smoking in the factory
Programme	Combination plan for goal achievement, non-repetitive	States activities and resources to be undertaken	Installation of a computer
Schedule	Time-table for activities	Specifies priority of work and time for each activity	Complete installation of computer within 3 months w.e.f. Jan, 1989.

Budget	Statement of expected results and resources to be used	Quantitative and time bound plan of action	Produce 10,000 tonnes of sugar next year
Project	Cluster of interrelated activities-a separate unit	Scheme for deployment of resources	Construction of a flyover

(*a*) Differences between policies and strategies

Sl.No.	Policies	Strategies
1	Guides to thinking and actions of those who make decisions	Provide direction in which human and physical resources will be deployed
2	Guidelines for making decisions in repetitive situations	Contingent decisions
3	Taken for problems about which facts are known. Only time of occurrence is not specific	Taken for problems where alternatives cannot be analysed in advance.
4	Implementation of policy can be delegated	Implementation of strategy cannot be delegated as it requires last-minute executive decision
5	Standing plan or long lasting	Non-repetitive plans, may need frequent revision
6	Not based specially on the moves of competitors	Formulated in the light of competitors' moves

(*b*) Differences between policy and procedure

Sl.No.	Policies	Procedures
1	General guides to thinking and decision-making	Operational guides to action
2	Expressions of management's attitude towards certain issues	Systematic ways of handling routine events
3	Leave room for executive discretion and judgement	Leave little room for reflection and deviation
4	Lay down broad area	Provide route through the area
5	Provide bridge between purpose and performance	Provide bridge between activities and outcomes
6	Provide norms for thinking and discretion. Broad, general and flexible	Detailed and rigid. More specific. Provide manner of doing something
7	Form part of strategies	Serve as tactical tools
8	Formulated mainly by top management	Laid down at middle and lower levels
9	Derived from objectives of the organisation	Specifies chronological sequence of steps. Derived from policies

(*c*) **Difference between Policies and Rules**

Sl.No.	Policies	Rules
1	A general statement	A most specific statement
2	Guide to decision-making	Guide to behaviour
3	Lays down management attitude	Indicates what should or should not be done
4	Flexible, may have some exceptions	Rigid, no exceptions or deviations
5	Provides discretion during implementation	Provide no scope for discretion

(*d*) **Distinction between Objectives and Policies**

Sl.No.	Objectives	Policies
1	Ends towards which all activities of an organisation are directed	Guidelines which facilitate the accomplishment of predetermined objectives
2	Determine what is to be done	Determine how the work is to be done
3	End-points of planning	Means by which objectives are to be achieved
4	Determined by top management	Formulated at top and middle levels
5	One objective may require more than one policy	Every policy related to one particular objective
6	Derived from philosophy of business	Derived from objectives
7	Indicate the destination	Provide the route
8	Basic to the very existence of an organisation	Not basic to existence

2.9. OBJECTIVES

2.9.1. Meaning

Every organization exists to achieve some purposes, which is called its objectives. Objectives are the results which management wants to achieve through the making and implementation of a plan.

2.9.2. Definition

> *"Objectives are goals established to guide the efforts of the Company and each of its components".*
>
> —**Luis Allen**

2.9.3. Nature/Characteristics of Objectives

1. An organization has multiple objectives. Objectives are numerous. Even the mission and broad major enterprise objectives are normally multiple. For example, profits, survival, growth, service to society etc. This multiplicity of objectives creates the problem of fixing priorities among different objectives and of harmonizing them.

2. Objectives have time Span. An organization must have short-term, middle term and long-term objectives. Short term and middle term objectives are means of achieving long-term objectives. All these objectives need to be integrated so that they reinforce each other.

3. Objectives are either tangible or intangible. Some of the objectives are tangible such as areas of market standing, productivity, and physical and financial resources are quantifiable values available. Other areas of objectives are not readily quantifiable and are completely intangible which are qualitative natures, such as manager's performance, worker's morale, public responsibility etc.

4. Objectives form a hierarchy. Objectives form a hierarchy, ranging from the broad aim to specific individual objectives. Generally, a top-level management of an organization assigning a part of a mission to a particular department. Then the mission is subdivided into few parts and assigned among sections and individuals. This process creates hierarchy of objectives. Objectives at all levels in the organization are interrelated and form a network.

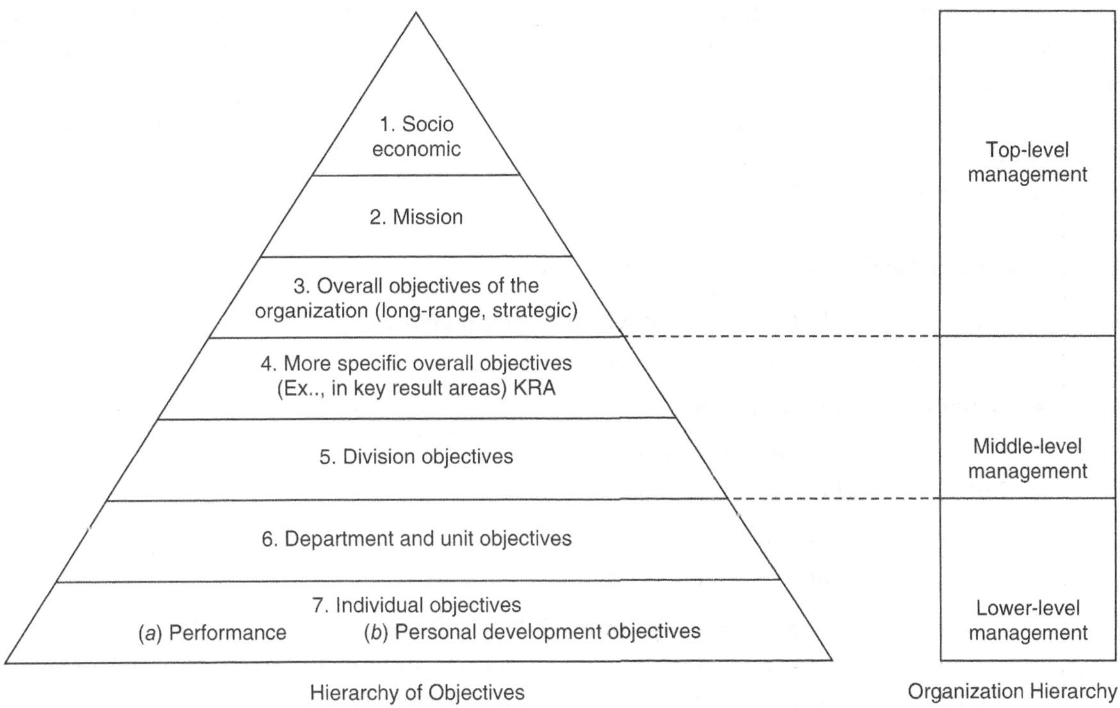

Relationship of Objectives and the Organizational Hierarchy

There are two types of approaches in which the hierarchy can be explained.

- Top-down approach
- Bottom-up approach.

In the top-down approach, the total organization is directed through corporate objective provided by the top level of management. In the bottom-up approach, the top-level management needs to have information from lower level in the form of objectives.

DECISION-MAKING

2.10. MEANING OF DECISION

A decision is a choice between two or more alternatives. This implies three things:

- *When managers make decisions they are choosing right one from alternatives,*
- *They are deciding what to do on the basis of some conscious, and*
- *Deliberate logic or judgment.*

A decision may be defined, in terms of commitment of resources—raw materials, machines, finance, time, efforts etc. in a particular channel of thinking and action.

For example, a decision to advertise the product, involves the time, effort, finance of the marketing department in preparation of advertisement programme, its implementation and reviewing its progress.

Whenever a manager takes a decision, his thinking and actions are involved in a particular direction. Whenever the decision is implemented, it implies commitment of precious organizational resources in that particular direction.

2.10.1. Types of Decisions

Decisions can be classified in a number of ways as shown below.

- Programmed and Non-programmed Decisions
- Major and Minor Decisions
- Routine and Strategic Decisions
- Individual and Group Decisions
- Simple and Complex Decisions
- Organizational and Personal Decisions

1. Programmed and Non-programmed Decisions. According to Herbert Simon, Programmed decisions are concerned with relatively routine and repetitive problems. Information on these problems is already available and can be processed in a preplanned manner. Such decision have short-term impact and are relatively simple. These types of decisions are made at lower level executives of management. These decisions require little thought and judgement. The decision-maker identifies the problem and applies the predetermined solution. For examples, granting leave to employees, purchase of raw materials, disciplinary action against late comers, determining salary payments to employees who have been ill, and so on.

Non-programmed decisions are novel and non-repetitive. Such decisions deal with unusual problems. It cannot be tackled in a predetermined manner. A high degree of executive judgement and deliberation is required to solve the problem. These types of decisions are made at higher-level management. For example, to locate a new branch office, development of a new product, and so on.

2. Major and Minor Decisions. Some decisions are considerably more important than others. For example, decision relating to the purchase of a new plant worth of ₹ 2 crores is a major decision. Top management may decide these decisions. On the other hand, purchase of spare parts for the machineries is a minor decision. The lower level management people may decide matter.

3. Routine and Strategic Decisions. Routine or operating decisions are of repetitive nature. They involve short-term commitment and have minor impact on the future of the organization. It relate to day-to-day operating of business. Usually standard procedures are established to make such decisions quickly. Routine decisions required little deliberation and money and are taken by managers as lower levels. For example, a supervisor can decide whether an employee is entitled to overtime pay or not, Provision for air conditioning, better lighting, parking facilities, cafeteria service, deputing employees to attend conferences, etc., are all routine decisions.

Strategic or policy decisions involve long-term commitments and large investments. These exercise a permanent influence on the future of the organization as a whole. Strategic decisions need much deliberation and judgement, because such basic decision deal with unique problems and policy issues. These types of decisions are made at top-level management. Launching a new product, location of a new plant, installations of computer system are examples of strategic decisions. Policy decisions are sometimes published as policy manual to guide operating managers.

4. Individual and Group Decisions. Individual decisions are taken by a single person at his capacity without consultation with any other persons whatsoever. Individual decisions are taken where the problem is of a routine nature where the analysis of variables is simple and where definite procedures to deal with the problem already exist.

Group decisions taken by a group of persons constituted for particular purpose. These decisions are generally important for the organization. Group decision making generally results in more realistic and well balanced decisions and encourages participative decision making. But it involves delay and makes it difficult to fix responsibility for such decisions. Decisions taken by Board of Directors or Committee are some examples of group decision.

Advantages of group decisions

- *Increased acceptance by those affected*

  The group's members mostly accept decisions made by a group and they help implement those decisions more readily.

- *Easier coordination*

  Decisions made by groups reduce the amount of coordination necessary to bring the decision into play.

- *Easier communication*

  Decisions made by groups reduce the amount of communication necessary to implement the decision.

- *More information processed*

  Because many individuals are involved, more data and information can be brought to bear on the decision.

Disadvantages of group decisions

- *Group decisions take longer*

  Groups take longer than individuals to make decisions.
- *Groups can be indecisive*

  Groups can drag on and never take decision because they can always blame other members of the group for lack of progress.
- *Groups can compromise*

  This can lead to decisions that satisfy the lowest common denominator. It can lead to groupthink or conformity to peer pressure.
- *Groups can be dominated*

  The highest status individual, if he chooses, can influence the group so that it notices his or her choices. This negates the advantages of group decision-making.

If the advantages are utilized and the disadvantages avoided, groups are better decision-making units than individuals.

Two approaches to group decision-making have recently been proposed as alternatives to the conventional interacting or discussion group. These two approaches, known as the nominal group technique and the Delphi technique are designed to avoid the disadvantages of groups and to utilize the advantages of groups for effective problem-solving.

Nominal Group Technique

This technique proceeds as under:

1. Members first silently and independently generate their ideas on a problem in writing.
2. They then present their ideas (one by one) to the group without discussion. The ideas are summarized and written on a black board.
3. The recorded ideas are then discussed for the purposes of clarification and evaluation.
4. Finally, each member silently gives his independent rating about various ideas through a system of voting. The group decision is the pooled outcome of individual votes.

Delphi Technique

In this technique, the group consists of persons who are physically dispersed and are anonymous to one another. They are asked to send their opinion on a topic through mail. For this purpose, they are first sent a carefully designed questionnaire. Their responses to the questionnaire are then summarized into a feedback report and sent back to them along with a second questionnaire which is designed to probe more deeply into the ideas generated in response to the first questionnaire. Generally, a final summary is developed on the basis of replies received the second time.

5. Simple and Complex Decisions. When variables to be considered for solving a problem are few, the decision is simple; when they are many, the decision is complex. When we combine these two types of decisions with the low or high certainty of their outcomes, we get four types of decisions.

- A decision in which the problem is simple and the outcome has a high degree of certainty. These are called ***mechanistic or routine decisions.***
- Decisions in which the problem is simple but the outcome has a low degree of certainty. These are called ***judgemental decisions***. Many decisions in the area of marketing, investment and personnel are of this type.
- Decisions in which the problem is complex but the outcome has a high degree of certainty. These are called ***analytical decision***. Many decisions in the area of production are of this type.
- A decision in which the problem is complex and the outcome has a low degree of certainty. These are called ***adaptive decision***. Changes in corporate plans and policies to meet the changes in environment and technology are decisions of this type.

6. Organizational and Personal Decisions. Organizational decisions are made to further development of organization. Managers make them in their official capacity as allocator of resources. These decisions are based on rationality, judgement and experience. Such decisions can be delegated to lower levels. These decisions affect the functioning of the organization. For example, decision relating to payment of dividend, alteration of authorized capital, adoption of new product technology etc.

Personal decisions are made by a single individual. Such decision can not be delegated. For example, decision to retire early, decision to resign the post, decision to marry and so on. Such decisions affect the personal life of a manager but may affect the organization indirectly or directly. For example, the decision of a manager to proceed on a long leave is a personal decision of the manager. But then, in interest of the organization he must depute some person for act on his behalf, till he returns.

2.10.2. Meaning of Decision-making

Decision-making is the process of choosing a course of action from among alternatives to achieve desired results.

2.10.3. Definition of Decision-making

Decision-making is a course of action chosen by a manager as the most effective means at his disposal for achieving goals and solving problems. —*Theo Haimann*

2.10.4. Relationship between Decision and Decision-making

Decision-making is a process; a decision is the outcome of this process.

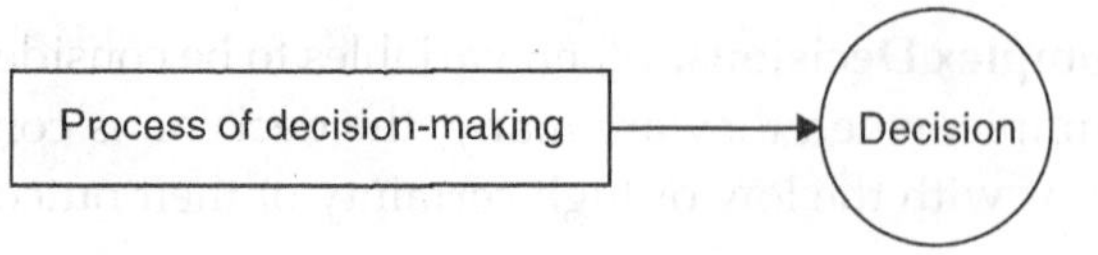

2.10.5. Steps in Decision-making Process

Following six steps involved in the process of decision-making:

- *Identify the problem.*
- *Diagnosing the problem*
- *Discover alternative course of action.*
- *Evaluate alternatives*
- *Select the best alternatives*
- *Implementing and follow-up of action.*

1. Identification of the Problem. The decision making process begins with the recognition of a problem that requires a decision. The problem may arise due to gap between present and desired state of affairs. The threats and opportunities created by environmental changes may also create decision problems. At this stage, a manager should identify and define the real problem. A problem well defined is half solved. In order to recognize the problem quickly, a manager must continuously monitor the decision-making environment,. Imagination, experience and judgement are required for detection of problems that require managerial decisions.

2. Diagnose the Problem. Diagnosing the real problem implies analyzing it in terms of its elements, its magnitude, its urgency, its courses, and its relation with other problems. In order to diagnose the problem correctly, a manager must obtain all pertinent facts and analyse them carefully. The most important part of diagnosing the problem of manufacturing costs and may start a cost reduction drive when the real problem is poor engineering design.

The problem may be analyzed in terms of the following:

- *Nature of the decision-routine or strategic*
- *Impact of the decision*
- *Futurity of the decision*
- *Periodicity of the decision, and*
- *Limiting or strategic factor relevant to the decision*

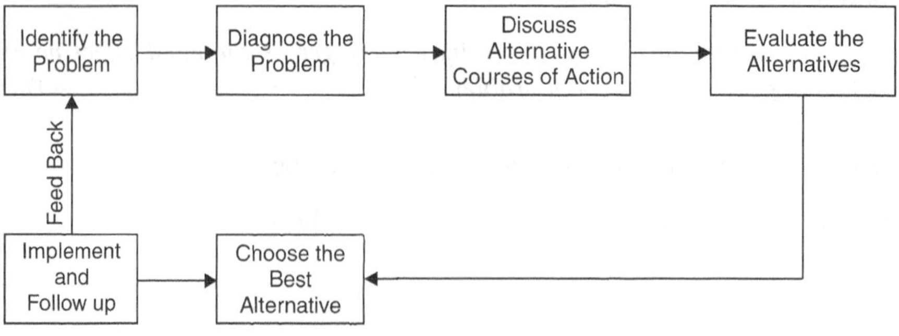

Decision-Making Process

3. Discover Alternatives. The next step is to search for the various possible alternatives. An executive should not jump on the first feasible alternative to solve the problem quickly. A wide range of alternatives increases the manager's freedom of choice. But it is advisible for the manager to limit himself to discover of those alternatives, which are strategic or critical to the problem. The ***Principle of the limiting factor*** should be followed for this purpose. According to Barnard, "Strategic factors refer to those that are most important in determining the action to be taken in solving a given problem." For example, in a decision to expand operations, capital or government control or size may be the limiting factors. "In choosing from among alternatives, the more an individual can recognize and solve those factors which are limiting or critical to the attainment of the desired goal, the more clearly and accurately he or she can select the most favourable alternative". The idea is to keep the range of alternatives within a manageable limit. Time and cost constraints should be kept in mind. Development of alternatives is a creative process requiring research and imagination. Management must ensure that the best alternatives are considered before a course of action is selected. Relevant information must be collected and analyzed for this purpose.

4. Evaluate Alternatives. Once the alternatives are discovered, the next stage is to evaluate or screen each feasible alternative. Evaluation is the process of measuring the positive and negative consequences of each alternative. Management must balance the costs against possible benefits. Considerable knowledge and judgement are required to measure the plus and minus points and to find out the net benefit of each alternative. Both quantitative and qualitative evaluation is needed to ensure that all tangible and intangible factors are taken into account. The element of risk involved in each alternative and the resources available for its implementation should also be considered. Management must set some criteria against which the alternatives can be evaluated.

Peter Drucker has suggested the following criteria to weigh the alternative courses of action:

(*a*) ***Risk:*** Degree of risk involved in each alternative.

(*b*) ***Economy of effort:*** Cost, time and effort involved in each alternative.

(*c*) ***Timing:*** Whether the problem is urgent.

(*d*) ***Limitation of resources:*** Physical, financial and human resources.

5. Select the Best Alternative. After evaluation, the optimum alternative is selected. Optimum alternative is the alternative that will maximize the results under given conditions. Choice of the best alternative is the most critical point in decision-making. The ability to select the best course of action from several possible alternatives separates the successful managers from the unsuccessful ones. Past experience, experimentation, research and analysis are useful in selecting the best alternative.

6. Implementation and Follow up. Once a decision is made it needs to be implemented. Implementation involves several steps. First, the decision should be communicated to those responsible for its implementation. Secondly, acceptance of the decision should be obtained. Thirdly, procedures and time sequence should be established for implementation. Necessary resources should be allocated and responsibility for specific tasks should be assigned to individuals.

The implementation of the decision should be constantly monitored. The effects of the decision should be judged through periodic progress reports. In case the feedback indicates that the decision is not yielding the desired results, necessary changes should be made in the decision or in its implementation.

Herbert Simon has identified three phases in the decision-making process:

(*i*) Intelligence activity involves a search for the conditions underlying the decision. It includes identification and diagnosis of the problem, definition of objectives and collection of information.

(*ii*) Decision activity is concerned with the generation and evaluation of alternative courses of action.

(*iii*) Choice activity implies selection of the best course of action. Post choice activity involves implementation of the decision.

Chapter 3 ORGANIZATION

3.1. MEANING OF ORGANIZATION

It refers to coordinate human resources with other resources such as material, machine, money etc. Once managers have established objectives and developed plans to achieve them, they must design and develop a human organization that will be able to carry out those plans successfully.

Sub functions of organizing functions are as follows: Functionalisation, divisionalisation, departmentation, delegation, decentralization, activity analysis, task allocation.

3.2. DEFINITION

"Organization refers to the structure, which results from identifying and grouping work, defining and delegating responsibility and authority, and establishing relationships."

—Louis Allen

"An organization is a social unit or human grouping, deliberately structured for the purpose of attaining specific goals."

—Amitai Etzioni

For example, corporation, Armies, Schools, Hospitals, etc. are the organizations. But tribes, Ethnic, and friendship group and families are not organization because they do not involve any significant amount of conscious planning or deliberate structuring.

3.3. NATURE OF ORGANIZATION/CHARACTERISTICS OF ORGANIZATION

The main characteristics of organization are as follows:

1. Common purpose. Every organization exist to accomplish some common goals. The structure must reflect these objectives as enterprise activities are derived from them. It is bound by common purpose.

2. Division of labour. The total work of an organisation is divided into function and sub-functions. This is necessary to avoid the waste of time, energy and resources, which arises when people have to constantly change from one work to another. It also provides benefits of specialisation.

3. Authority structure. There is an arrangement of positions into a graded series. The authority of every position is defined. It is subordinate to the position above it and superior to the one below it. This chain of superior-sub-ordinate relationships is known as chain of command.

4. People. An organisation is basically a group of persons. Therefore, activity groupings and authority provision must take into account the limitations and customs of people. People constitute the dynamic human element of an organisation.

5. Communication. Every organisation has its own channels of communication. Such channels are necessary for mutual understanding and co-operation among the members of an organisation.

6. Co-ordination. There is a mechanism for coordinating different activities and parts of an organisation so that it functions as an integrated whole. Co-operative effort is a basic feature of organisation.

7. Environment. As organisation functions in an environment comprising economic, social, political and legal factors. Therefore, the structure must be designed to work efficiently in a changing environment. It cannot be static or mechanistic.

8. Rules and Regulations. Every organisation has some rules and regulations for orderly functioning of people. These rules and regulations may be in writing or implied from customary behaviour.

3.4. PRINCIPLES OF ORGANIZATION

In order to develop a sound and efficient organisation structure, there is need to follow certain principles. In the words of E.F.L. Brech, if there is to be a systematic approach to the formulation of organisation structure, there ought to be a body of accepted principles. These principles are as follows.

1. Objectives. The objectives of the enterprise influence the organisation structure and hence the objectives of the enterprise should first be clearly defined. Then every part of the organisation should be geared to the achievement of these objectives.

2. Specialisation. Effective organisation must promote specialisation. The activities of the enterprise should be divided according to functions and assigned to persons according to their specialisation.

3. Span of control. As there is a limit to the number of persons that can be supervised effectively by one boss, the span of control should be as far as possible, the minimum. That means, an executive should be asked to supervise a reasonable number of subordinates only say six.

4. Exception. As the executives at the higher levels have limited time, only exceptionally complex problems should be referred to them and the subordinates at lower levels should deal with routine matters. This will enable the executives at higher levels to devote time to more important and crucial issues.

5. Scalar principle. This principle is sometimes known as the ***chain of command***. The line of authority from the chief executive at the top to the first-line supervisor at the bottom must be clearly defined.

6. Unit of command. Each subordinate should have only one superior whose command he has to obey. Dual subordination must be avoided, for it causes uneasiness, disorder, indiscipline and undermining of authority.

7. Delegation. Proper authority should be delegated at the lower levels of organisation also. The authority delegated should be equal to responsibility, i.e., each manager should have enough authority to accomplish the task assigned to him.

8. Responsibility. The superior should be held responsible for the acts of his subordinates. No superior should be allowed to avoid responsibility by delegating authority to his subordinates.

9. Authority. The authority is the tool by which a manager is able to accomplish the desired objective. Hence, the authority of each manager must be clearly defined. Further, the authority should be equal to responsibility.

10. Efficiency. The organisation structure should enable the enterprise to function efficiently and accomplish its objectives with the lowest possible cost.

11. Simplicity. The organisation structure should be as simple as possible the organisation levels should, as far as possible, be minimum. A large number of levels of organisation means difficulty of effective communication and coordination.

12. Flexibility. The organisation should be flexible, should be adaptable to changing circumstances and permit expansion and replacement without dislocation and disruption of the basic design.

13. Balance. There should be a reasonable balance in the size of various departments, between centralization and decentralization, between the principle of span of control and the short chain of command, and among all types of factors as human, technical and financial.

14. Unity of Direction. There should be one objective and one plan for a group of activities having the same objective. Unity of direction facilitates unification and coordination of activities at various levels.

15. Personal ability. As people constitute an organisation, there is need for proper selection, placement and training of staff. Further, the organisation structure must ensure optimum use of human resources and encourage management development programmes.

3.5. ORGANIZATION PROCESS

The term organization is used in two different senses. In the first sense it is used to denote the process of organizing.

In the second sense it is used to denote the result of that process, namely, the organization structure (departmentation).

Using it in the first sense, organization is the process of defining and grouping the activities of the enterprise and establishing the authority relationships among them. In performing the organizing function, the manager differentiates and integrates the activities of his organization. By differentiation is meant the process of departmentalization or segmentation of activities on the basis of some homogeneity. Integration is the process of achieving unity of effort among the various departments (segments or subsystems).

Organization procedure consists of six steps.

1. Consideration of objectives. The first step in organizing is to know the objectives of the enterprise. Objectives determine the various activities, which need to be performed, and the type of organisation, which needs to be built for this purpose. Management writers, such as Alfred D. Chandler refer to this phenomenon as one in which "structure follows strategy." For example, the structure required for an army is different from the structure required for a business enterprise. In view of this, consideration of objectives is the first step in the process of organization.

2. Grouping of activities into departments. After the consideration of objectives, the next step is to identify the activities necessary to achieve them and to group the closely related and similar activities into divisions and departments. For example, the activities of a manufacturing concern may be grouped into such departments as production, marketing, financing and personnel. In addition, the activities of each department may be further classified and placed under the charge of different sections of that department. For example, in the production department, separate sections may be created for research, industrial engineering, etc. The topic of departmentalization has been dealt with in a separate section in this chapter.

3. Deciding which departments will be key departments. Key departments are those, which are rendering key activities, *i.e.*, activities essential for the fulfillment of goals. Such key departments demand key attention. Other departments exist merely to serve them. Experience suggests that where key departments are not formally identified, the attention of top management is focused on the minor issues raised by vocal managers. This is known as the ***"decibel system"*** of management. The key departments should be placed directly under higher management.

Which department needs to be emphasized how much will depend, of course, on the company's objectives and the way it seeks to be distinctive. For example, a company, which believes that advertising is a primary key to success will set up a separate advertising department, that reports directly to the president. But another company, which considers it much less important, may only create separate section for it under its sales department. Similarly, product development, which is treated as a key department in all chemical and pharmaceutical companies, with those in charge reporting directly to the president, may be treated only as a section of the production department in textile companies. The importance of an activity may also grow with times. Thus, personnel management, which was hitherto considered less important, is now treated as important activity and has risen in organizational status.

4. Determining levels of which various types of decision are to be made. After deciding the relative importance of various departments, the levels at which various major and minor decisions are to be made must be determined. Each firm must decide for it as to how much decentralization of authority and responsibility it wants to have. Extreme decentralization may lead to loss of control and effective coordination as a result of which the firm as a whole may fail to achieve its overall objectives. Extreme centralization, on the other hand, may lead to wrong decision sat wrong times and complete breakdown of the morale of employees.

5. Determining the span of management. The next step to be taken in designing a structure is to determine the number of subordinates who should report directly to each executive. The narrower the span, the taller would be the structure with several levels of management. This will complicate communication and increase the payroll. For these reasons, a flat structure is generally desirable.

6. Setting up a coordination mechanism. Emphasizing the importance of coordination in an organization, Peter Drucker says that an organization is like a tune. It is not constituted of individual sounds but of the relation between them. As individuals and departments carry out their specialized activities, the overall goals of the organization may become submerged or conflicts among organization members may develop. For example, production managers in a manufacturing company may press for a standardized product line to hold down costs, when the larger interests of the company may be best served by a diversified product line. In a university, various schools or departments may begin to compete for limited funds.

3.6. FORMAL AND INFORMAL ORGANIZATIONS

3.6.1. Formal Organization

A formal organization typically consists of a classical hierarchical structure in which positions; responsibility, authority, accountability and the line of command are clearly defined and established. It is a system of well-defined jobs with a prescribed pattern of communication, coordination and delegation of authority.

According to Allen, "The formal organization is a system of well defined jobs, each bearing a definite measure of authority, responsibility, and accountability".

Formal organization must be flexible. Each and every person is assigned the duties and given the required amount of authority and responsibility to carryout the job. It creates co-ordination between workers to achieve common goal. The inter relationship of staff members can be shown in the organization chart and manuals under formal organization.

3.6.1.1. Characteristics of Formal Organization

- It is flexible and properly planned.
- It is based on principle of division of labour and efficiency in operations.
- It concentrates more on the performance of jobs and not on the individuals performing the jobs.

- Organization charts are usually drawn.
- Coordination among members and their control are well specified through processes, procedures, rules etc.
- The responsibility and accountability at all levels of organization should be clearly defined.
- Unity of command is normally maintained.

3.6.1.2. Advantages of Formal Organization

- Since the definite boundaries of each worker are clearly defined, the conflict among the workers is automatically reduced.
- Overlapping of responsibility is easily avoided.
- More stable organization can be ensured. It makes the organization less dependent on one man.
- A sense of security arises from classification of the task.
- It motivates the employees.

3.6.2. Informal Organization

It refers to the pattern of activities, interactions and human relationships, which emerge spontaneously due to social and psychological forces operating at the work place. It arises naturally on the basis of friendship or some common interest, which may or may not be related with work. It is an unintended and non-planned network of unofficial and social patterns of human relationships. Informal organization represents the pattern of interpersonal and intergroup relations that develop within the formal organization. For example, the typists working in different department may form an informal group due to similarity of work. Common language, common habits, common hobby may also lead to informal groups. It is an unofficial and social pattern of human interactions.

According to Chester Barnard, "Informal organization is joint personal activity without conscious common purpose through contributing to joint results".

3.6.2.1. Characteristics of Informal Organization

- It arises without any external cause *i.e.,* voluntarily. It is a natural outcome at the work place.
- It is created on the basis of some similarity among the members. The bases of similarity may be age, sex, place of birth, caste, religion, likings/dislikings etc.
- Informal organization has no place in the organization chart.
- It is one of the parts of total organization.
- It has no structure and definiteness to the informal organization.
- A person may become member of several informal organizations at the same time.
- The rules and traditions of informal organization are not written but are commonly followed.

3.6.2.2. Advantages of Informal Organization

- Since informal organization gives satisfaction to the workers, it motivates workers and also maintains the stability of the work.
- It fills up the gaps and deficiency of the formal organization.
- It fills up the gaps among the abilities of the managers.
- The presence of informal organization encourages the executives to plan the work correctly and act accordingly.
- It is one of the useful channel or communication.

3.6.2.3. Disadvantages of Informal Organization

- Informal organizations may function in ways that are counter productive. They may stand in the way of organization achieving the objectives.
- It indirectly reduces the effort of management to promote greater productivity.
- It spreads rumour among the workers regarding the functioning of the organization unnecessarily.

3.6.3. Difference between Formal and Informal Organization

Sl.No.	Point of view	Formal Organization	Informal Organization
1	Origin	It is created deliberately and consciously by the frames of the organization	It is created spontaneously and naturally
2	Purpose	It is created for achieving legitimate objectives of the organization	It is created by the members of the organization for social and psychological satisfaction
3	Nature	Planned and official	Unplanned and unofficial
4	Size	It may quite large	It may be small in size
5	Nature of groups	It may be stable and continue for a very long period of time	It is quite unstable in nature
6	Number of groups	More	Less
7	Structure	Definite structure, mechanical and rational	Structureless, impersonal and emotional
8	Authority	Authority flows from top to bottom	It may flows upward to downwards from or horizontally
9	Communication	Communication normally flows through the prescribed chain of command	Communications pass through the informal channels which do not have one single form
10	Control process	Rigid rules and regulations	Group norms and values

3.7. DEPARTMENTATION

3.7.1. Meaning of Departmentation

Grouping of activities is an essential step in designing an organisation structure. Grouping of activities into departments, division or other homogeneous units is known as departmentation. Departmentation or departmentalisation is the process of grouping tasks into jobs, the combining of jobs into effective work groups and the combining of groups into identifiable segments or departments. It involves horizontal differentiation of activities in an enterprise. A department is a division, branch, regiment or some other organisational unit over which a manager has authority for performance of task. Thus, departmentation is the process of dividing the work of organisation into departments or other manageable units.

3.7.2. Need and Importance of Departmentation

The basic purpose of departmentation is to make the size of each departmental unit manageable and to secure advantages of specialisation. Departmentation is necessary on account of the following reasons.

1. Specialization. Departmentation enables an organisation to avail of the benefits of specialisation. When every department looks after one major function, expertise is developed and efficiency of operations increases.

2. Expansion. One manager can supervise and direct only a few subordinates. Grouping of activities and personnel into departments makes it possible for the enterprise to expand and grow. If there is no departmentation, the size of the organisation will be restricted to a manager's span of control.

3. Autonomy. Departmentation results in the division of the enterprise into semi-autonomous units. In these units, every manager is given adequate freedom. The feeling of autonomy provides job satisfaction and motivation, which in turn lead to higher efficiency of operations.

4. Fixation of Responsibility. Departmentation enables each person to know the specific part he is to play in the total organisation. It provides a basis for building up loyalty and commitment. The responsibility for results can be defined more precisely and an individual can be held accountable for performance.

5. Appraisal. Appraisal of managerial performance becomes easier when specific tasks are assigned to departmental personnel. The sources of information, the skills and competence required for total managerial decisions can be located.

6. Management Development. Departmentation facilitates communication, coordination and control. It simplifies the training and development of executives by providing them opportunity to take independent decisions and to exercise initiative.

7. Administrative Control. Departmentation is a means of dividing the large and complex organisation into small and flexible administrative units. Grouping of activities and personnel into manageable units facilitates administrative control. Standards of performance for each and every department can be precisely determined. Excessive departmentation may result in several organisational problems such as erosion of the line of command, multiple accountability, dysfunctional conflicts and difficulty of co-ordination and control.

3.7.3. Basis (or) Types of Departmentation (Patterns of Grouping Activities)

The following patterns may be used for grouping activities into departments.

1. Departmentation by Functions.
2. Departmentation by Products.
3. Departmentation by Territory.
4. Departmentation by Customer.
5. Departmentation by Process or Equipment.
6. Departmentation by Time.
7. Departmentation by Numbers.
8. Composite Departmentation.

1. Functional Departmentation. Under functional departmentation each major or basic function is organized as a separate department. Basic or organic functions are the functions the performance of which is vital and essential to the survival of the organization. For example, production, marketing, financing and personnel are basic functions in a manufacturing enterprise. On the other hand, in a retail stores buying, selling and finance are the major functions. If necessary, a major function may be divided into minor or sub-functions. For instance, activities in the production department may be classified into quality control, processing of materials and repairs and maintenance. Thus, the process of functional differentiation may take place through successive levels in the hierarchy. The process can continue as long as there exists a sound basis for further differentiation. Functional departmentation is the most widely used basis for grouping activities. It exists almost in every organization at some level.

Advantages

- It is the most logical, time proven and natural form of departmentation.
- It provides occupational specialization, which makes optimum utilization of manpower.

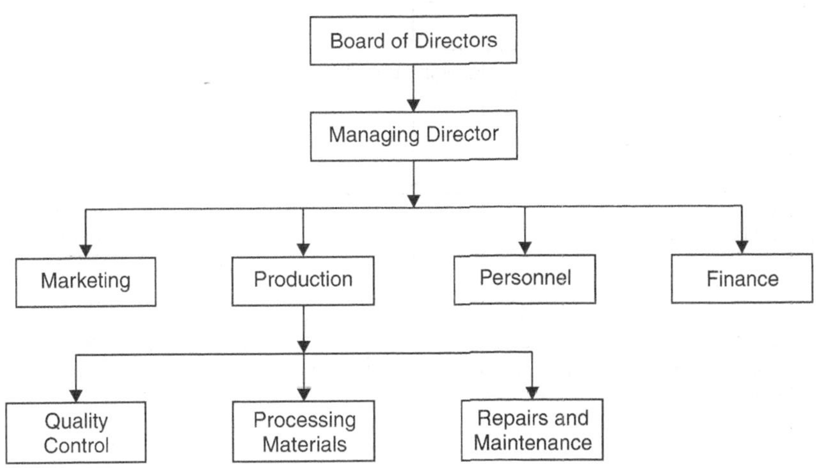

- It ensures the performance of all activities necessary for achieving organizational objectives. It gives status to major functions.
- It facilitates delegation of authority.
- It enables top management to exercise effective control over a limited number of functions.
- It eliminates costly duplication of effort.
- It simplifies training because managers have to be experts only in a narrow range of skills.

Disadvantages

- There is too much emphasis on specialization. When each employee specializes only in a small part of the job, cannot develop a balanced attitude towards the job as whole.
- There may be conflicts between departments as the responsibilities are interdependent and cannot always be clearly delineated.
- Functional departments may grow in size to justify their costs. Managers may try to build the functional empires.
- It does not offer a good training ground for the overall development of a manager. The manager gains expertise in handing problems of his particular department only.

2. Product Departmentation. In product or service departmentation, every major product is organized as a separate department. Each department looks after the production, sales and finance of one product. Product departmentation is useful when product expansion and diversification, manufacturing and marketing characteristics of the product are of primary significance. It is generally employed when the product line is relatively complex and diverse requiring specialized knowledge and a great deal of capital is required for plant and equipment such as in automobile and electronic industries. Several companies in India, such as Hindustan Lever Ltd manufacturing detergents, toiletries, chemicals and agro-based products. Richardson and Hindustan manufacturing a range of vicks products, Clearasil cream and soap and Johnson and Johnson manufacturing a range of products for children and surgical sutures have product-based departments. Each division may be sub-divided into production, sales, finance and personnel activities.

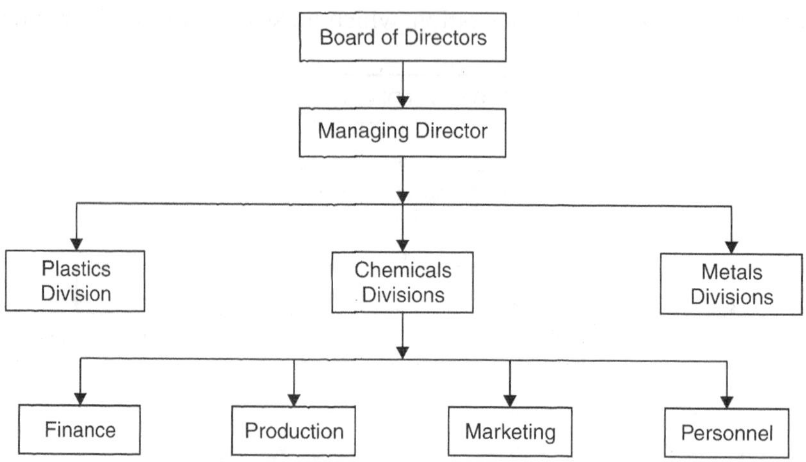

Advantages

- Product department can reduce the problem of coordination between production and sales activities. All activities concerning a particular product line are integrated together.
- It focuses individual attention on each product line, which facilitates product expansion and diversification.
- It permits full use of specialized production facilities. Personal skills and specialized knowledge of product managers can be fully utilized.
- The performance of each product division and its contribution to overall results can be easily evaluated.
- It is more flexible and adaptable.
- This form enables top management to compare the performance of different products and invest more resources in profitable products and withdraw resources from unprofitable ones.

Disadvantages

- There is a duplication of physical facilities and functions. Each product divisions maintain its own specialized facilities and personnel due to which operating costs may be high.
- Advantages of centralization of certain activities like financing, accounting, industrial relations etc. are not available.
- There may be underutilization of plant capacity when the demand for a particular product is not adequate.
- It creates the problem of effective control over product divisions by the top management.

3. Territorial Departmentation. Territorial departmentation is very useful to a large-scale enterprise whose activities are geographically spread over a wide area. Banks, insurance companies, transport companies, distribution agencies and Indian railways are examples of such enterprise. Under territorial or geographical departmentation, activities are divided into zones, divisions and branches. It is obviously not possible for one functional manager to manage efficiently such widely separated activities. This makes it necessary to appoint regional managers for different regions.

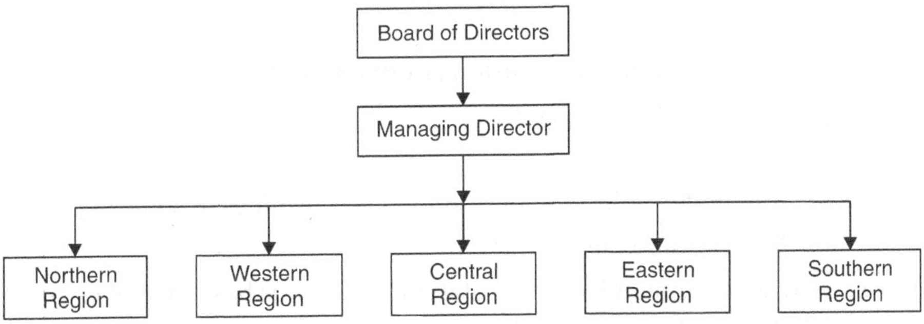

Advantages

- It motivates each regional head to achieve high performance.
- It provides each regional head an opportunity to adapt to his local situation and customer need with speed and accuracy.

- It affords valuable top management training and experience to middle level executives.
- It enables the organization to take advantage of locational factors, such as availability of raw materials, labour, market, etc.
- It enables the organization to compare regional performances and invest more resources and profitable regions and withdraw resources from unprofitable once.

Disadvantages

- It gives rise to duplication of various activities. Many routine and service functions performed by all the regional units can be performed centrally by the head office very economically.
- Various regional units may become so engrossed in short run competition, themselves that they may forget the overall interest of the total organization.

4. Customer Departmentation. Under this basis of departmentation, activities are grouped according to the type of customers. For instance, a large cloth stores may be divided into wholesale, retail and export divisions. This type of departmentation is useful for bans, departmental stores, etc., which sell a product or service to a number of distinct and clearly defined customer groups. Each department specializes in serving a particular class of customers. For example, an educational institution may have separate departments for day, evening and correspondence courses to impart education to full time students, locally employed students and outstation students respectively.

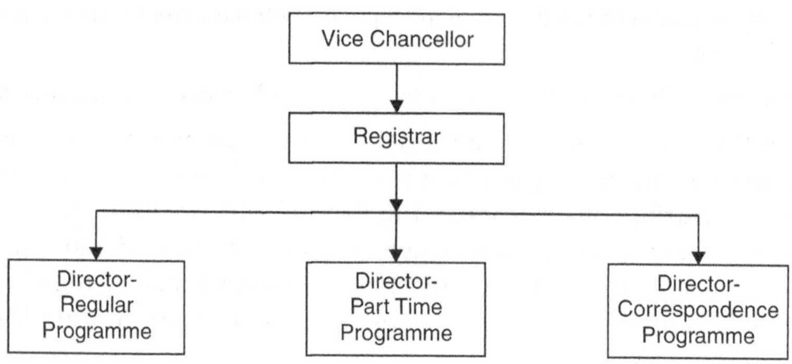

Advantages

- It ensures full attention to major customer groups, and
- It helps the company to earn goodwill.

Disadvantages

- It may result in under utilization of resources and facilities in some departments,
- There may be duplication of facilities.

5. Processes (or) Equipment Departmentation. Under this basis, activities are grouped on the basis of production process or equipments involved. This is generally used in a manufacturing enterprise and at lower levels of organization. For example, a textile mill may be organized into ginning, spinning, weaving and dyeing departments. Similarly, a printing press may consist of composing, proof reading, printing and binding departments. Such departmentation may also be used in engineering and oil industries. The main object is to achieve efficiency and economy of operations.

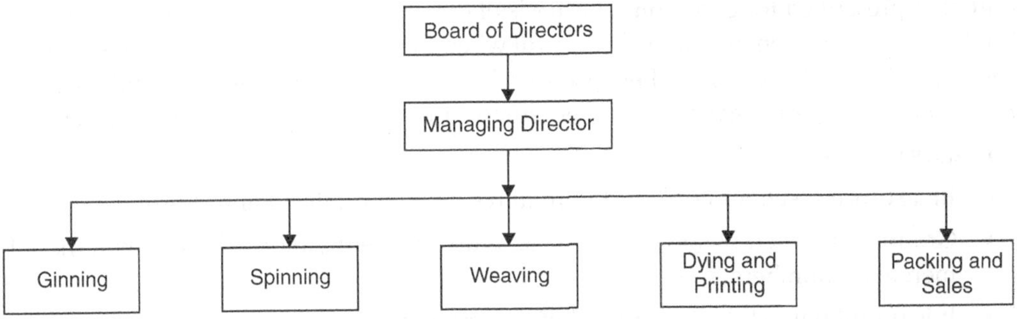

Advantages

- There is clear-cut technical division of work.
- This ensures specialization and facilitates training of junior executives.
- It is possible to appoint persons with special education and experience for each process.
- Location of similar type of machines in one place results in economies in costs of repairs and maintenance.

Disadvantages

- Coordination of departments is difficult.
- As the responsibility for profits is at the top, the departments do not focus their efforts on costs and its reduction.
- More specialists are essential to each process.
- It does not give training to staff members and there is a lack of overall development.
- Conflicts among managers of different processes may arise.

6. Time Departmentation. Under this basis activities are grouped on the basis of the time of their performance. For example, a factory operating twenty-four hours may have three departments, one each for morning, day and night shifts. The idea is to obtain the advantages of people specialized to work in a particular shift.

Advantages

- Service can be rendered around the clock basis.
- It is possible to use processes that cannot be interrupted, those that require a continuing cycle.
- Expensive capital equipment can be used effectively. *i.e.*, 24 hrs/day.

Disadvantages

- Supervising may be lacking during the night shift.
- Some people may feel difficult to switch from a day shift to a night shift and vice-versa.
- As it has several shifts, it may create problems in coordination and communication.
- Payment of overtime rates can increase the cost of the product.

7. Departmentation by Numbers. In case of departmentation by simple numbers, activities are grouped on the basis of their performance by a certain number of persons. For example, in the army soldiers are grouped into squads, battalions, companies, brigades and regiments on the basis of the number prescribed for each unit. This basis of departmentation is used at the lower levels of hierarchy. Departmentation by numbers is useful when the work is repetitive and unskilled, where manpower is the most important, where group efforts are more important than individual efforts and where the group performance can be measured. It is useful only at the lowest level.

Disadvantages

- In advanced technology world, it requires more specialized and different skills.
- Groups composed of specialized persons are frequently more efficient than those based merely on numbers.
- It is useful only at the lower level of the organization.

8. Composite (or) Combine Departmentation. Departmentation is not an end in itself but a means for achieving organizational objectives. Each basis of departmentation has its own merits and demerits. Therefore, the relative advantages and limitations of various types of departmentation should be analyzed in the light of the needs and circumstances of the particular enterprise. That basis of departmentation is the best, which facilitates the achievement of organizational objectives most economically and efficiently.

In practice, no single pattern is ideal to suit all situations. Therefore, no single basis is followed for grouping activities. Rather, most of the big enterprises follow a composite or combination of several bases. For example, an organization manufacturing agricultural machinery may follow product as the base (tractor department, appliance department, generator department) at the primary level (*i.e.*, the level immediately below the chief executive), territory as the base at the intermediate level and function as the base at the ultimate level. This is shown as follows.

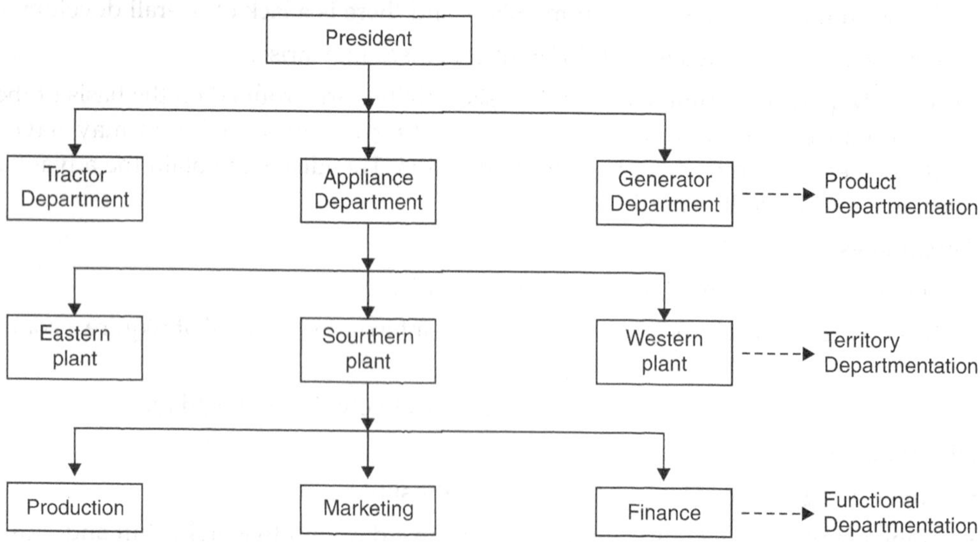

Matrix Organization

Matrix organization is another form of combined base organization, which is becoming very popular nowadays. Matrix organization is otherwise called ***Lattice pattern or Grid organization.*** In this form of organization, two types of departmentalization such as functional and product departmentalization exists simultaneously. Functional departments are a permanent fixture of the matrix organization; they retain authority for the overall operations of their respective units. Product departments or project teams, on the other hand, are created as the need for them arises that is, when a specific programme requires a high degree of technical skill in a concentrated period of time. Members of a project team are assembled from the functional departments and are placed under the direction of a project manager. The manager for each project is responsible and accountable for its success; thus he has authority over the other team members for the duration of the project. On the completion of the project, the team members of the team, including the project manager revert back to their respective departments until the next assignment to a project.

This form is now used in a variety of organizations, such as engineering companies executing turn-key projects, hospitals, universities, etc. hospitals now have both functionally organized departments (such as X-Ray, medicine, orthopedics, etc.) and latterly organized patient care teams. Universities have both functionally organized academic departments and specialized inter disciplinary programmes (such as MBA).

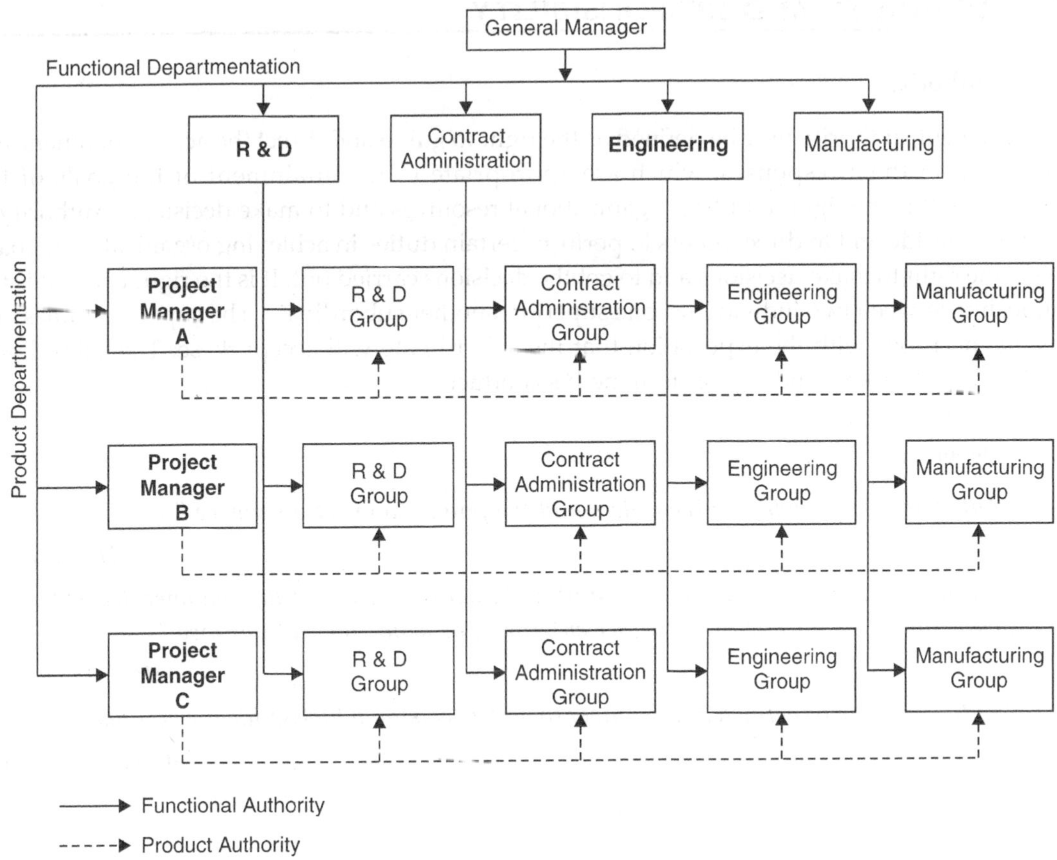

Merits

- The problem of coordination, which plagues most functional designs, is minimized here because the project manager acts as an integrator to relate personnel from diverse discipline.
- There is a reservoir of specialists, which ensures availability of expertise to all projects on the basis of their needs.
- There is economy in cost–each project is assigned only the number of people it needs, thus avoiding unnecessary surplus.
- There is an effective information decision system, which enables members to respond quickly to the change in project needs.

Demerits

- It violates the traditional principle of unity of command
- It fosters conflict because of the heterogeneity of team members.
- Matrix structure may be expensive. The dual chain command may cause management costs to double.

3.8. AUTHORITY AND RESPONSIBILITY

3.8.1. Authority

In management, authority may be defined as the right to guide and direct the actions of others and to secure from them responses, which are appropriate to the attainment of the goals of the organization. It is the right to utilize organizational resources and to make decisions. Authority is the right to decide and to direct others to perform certain duties in achieving organizational goals. It refers the right to make decisions and to get the decisions carried out. It is the right to act. It is the relationship between two individuals–one superior, another subordinate. The superior frames and transmits decisions with the expectation that the subordinate will accept these. The subordinate executes such decisions and they determine his conduct.

3.8.1.1. Definition

"Authority is the right to give orders and the power to exact obedience."

—Henry Fayol

"Authority is the power to command other to act or not to act in a manner deemed by the possessor of the authority to further enterprise or departmental purpose."

—Koontz & O'Donnell

"Authority may be defined as the power to make decision which guide the actions of others."

—Herbert A. Simon

3.8.2. Responsibility

Responsibility always arises from the superior-subordinate relationship. The essence of responsibilities is obligation. If a person is entrusted with any work, he should be held responsible for the work that he completes. Responsibility is the obligation to do something. In other words, responsibility is the obligation to perform the tasks, functions or assignments of the organization to achieve certain results.

3.8.2.1. Definition

> *"Responsibility may be defined as the obligation of a subordinate, to whom duty has been assigned to perform the duty."*
>
> —*Koontz & O'Donnel,*
>
> *"Responsibility is the obligation of an individual to perform assigned duties to the best of his ability under the direction of his executive leader."*
>
> —*R.C. Davis*
>
> *"Responsibility is the obligation of a subordinate to perform the duty as required by his superior."*
>
> —*Theo Haimann*

3.8.3. Distinction between Authority and Responsibility

Distinction	Authority	Responsibility
Meaning	Authority is a right vested in a managerial position; which enable the manager to command subordinates.	Responsibility is a duty or obligation owed by a subordinate to the superior, from whom the former derives authority–for the proper discharge of the assigned job.
Nature	It is primary	It is secondary or conditional. It is a corollary of authority; and cannot exist independently.
Flow	Authority flows from top to bottom via the management hierarchy.	Responsibility follows a reverse course. It proceeds in an anti-hierarchical manner from subordinate to superior.
Location	It is formal and impersonal. It is vested in managerial positions; and not in managers in their personal capacities.	It is personal in nature. It is owed by Persons to their superiors. It is not vested in managerial positions.
Delegation	It can be delegated by superiors to their subordinates for organizational purposes.	It cannot be delegated.
Termination	It granted to a manager can be terminated by the superior.	It cannot be terminated; at least for the acts for which a person is already responsible to his superior.

3.8.4. Power

Power is the ability to influence or to cause a person to perform an act. Power refers to the ability or capacity to influence the behaviour or attitudes of other individuals. A superior's power may be considered as his ability to cause subordinates to do what the superior wishes them to do.

3.8.4.1. Definition

> *"Power is the probability that one actor within the relationship will be in a position to carry out his own despite resistance."*
> —*Max Weber*

3.8.4.2. Types of Power

John R.P. French and Bertram Ravan have identified five basic types of power. The first three types such as reward, coercive, and legitimate power are associated with a manager's position. The last two-referent and expert power are part of person, not the position.

- *Reward power:* It arises from the ability of the people to grant rewards. The reward generally includes salary increment, promotion, favourable job assignment, praise and recognition.
- *Coercive power:* It is based on the manager's ability to punish for not complying with orders. It includes demotions, fines and threats of suspension or termination.
- *Legitimate power:* It is normally arises from position, which is legitimate. The higher a manager is in the hierarchy, the greater his legitimate power.
- *Referent power:* It refers to the power enjoyed by some people because of their integrity, charisma and popularity. A movie star or a military hero might posses such power.
- *Expert power:* It is based on possessing valued knowledge or special skills. A manager who possesses such knowledge or skill has power over others who do not. A famous doctors, advocates and professionals enjoy such power.

3.8.4.3. Distinction between Authority and Power

The objective of both authority and power is common, i.e., to influence the behaviour of others. But there are following important differences between authority and power.

Sl.No.	Authority	Power
1.	Right to do something	Ability to do something
2.	Derived from organization position-institutional	Derived from many sources–personal
3.	Always flows downward-can be delegated	Flows in all directions-cannot be delegated
4.	Legitimate-resides in the position	May be illegitimate or extra constitutional
5.	Narrow term-one source or subset of power	Broad concept-can achieve results when authority fails
6.	Visible from organization chart. It is institutionalized power	Not visible from organization chart

3.8.5. Line and Staff Authority

In line authority, a superior exercises direct command over a subordinate. It is represented by the standard chain of command that starts with the board of directors and extends down through the various levels in the hierarchy to the point where the basic activities of the organization are carried out.

The nature of staff authority is merely advisory. A staff officer has the authority of ideas only. The information, which a staff officer furnishes, or the plans he recommends flow upward to his line superior who decides whether they are to be transformed into action. For example, a market researcher who gathers and analyses data on marketing problems and advises the marketing manager on demand for new products; an industrial engineer who prepares layout plans of plant equipment, production methods and operating standards based on time studies and forwards them for the acceptance of the production manager; an internal auditor who checks the accuracy of accounting records and suggests to the head of the accounting department; a personnel officer who advises the personnel manager on all dealings with unions and so on.

Levels of authority of a staff man

At the lowest level, consultation of a staff man for his ideas by the line head is purely voluntary. The line head may or may not consult him. In fact, at this level his persuasive ability, status, backing or technical expertise determines the extent of his influence over others. At the next higher level, consultation is made compulsory for each department. Under this arrangement, the staff man must be consulted before action is taken. Line people cannot ignore him. The next higher level of staff man's authority is one where he is granted concurring authority, so that the line people can take no action until he agrees to it. Thus, no finished parts may move to the next stage of production until okayed by the quality control inspector, no new employee may be hired by a department head until approved by the personnel manager and so on are an examples of level of authority of a staff man. Under this arrangement, if the staff and the line people do not agree, an appeal is made to the next senior man in the hierarchy. The high-level authority people can give direct orders to people in other department outside his formal chain of command instead of making recommendations to them.

3.8.6. Delegation of Authority

3.8.6.1. Meaning

Delegation means assigning work to others and giving them authority to do it. It involves granting the right to decision-making in certain defined areas and charging the subordinates with responsibility for carrying out the assigned job.

3.8.6.2. Definition

> *"Delegation of authority is the process of manager follows in dividing the work assigned to him so that he performs that part which only he, because of his unique organizational placement, can perform effectively and so that he can get others to help with what remains."*
>
> *—Louis A. Allen*

3.8.6.3. Process of delegation

The process of delegation consists of the following aspects

- Assignment of duties
- Granting of authority
- Creation of accountability

1. **Assignment of duties.** The process of delegation starts with dividing the work into suitable parts. The manager has to decide what part of the work he will be transferred to his subordinates. Then he assigns the duties to subordinates indicating what he wants the subordinates to do.
2. **Granting of authority.** Duties cannot be performed without granting of the necessary authority. So the subordinates are given the requisite authority such as the use of resources, take necessary actions etc. to perform the given job.
3. **Creation of accountability.** Accountability is the obligation to carry out the responsibility with the help of authority in relation to the job entrusted. The subordinate to whom authority is delegated is also made accountable for the proper performance of the job entrusted to him.

3.8.6.4. Guidelines for effective delegation

1. Before delegating authority, make the nature and scope of the task clear
2. Assign authority proportionate to the task.
3. Make the subordinate clearly understand the limits of his authority.
4. Give the subordinate some positive incentives who are accepting responsibility.
5. Train the subordinate properly. First be in front of him for checkup and guidance and the be at his back to follow his performance.
6. Create climate of mutual trust and good will. The subordinate will work much better if he has the freedom to commit honest mistakes.
7. Do not make the subordinate accountable to more than one superior.
8. Let there be more overlaps or splits in delegation.

3.8.6.5. Advantages of delegation

1. It enables the managers to distribute their workload to others. By reducing the workload for routine matters, they can concentrate one or more important policy matters.
2. Delegation facilitates quick decisions because the authority to make decisions lies near the point of action. Subordinate need not approach the boss every time for a decision arises.
3. Delegation helps to improve the job satisfaction, motivation and morale of subordinates. It helps to satisfy their needs for recognition, responsibility and freedom.

4. By clearly defining the authority and responsibility of subordinates manager can maintain healthy relationship with them. Delegation increases interaction and understanding among managers and subordinates.
5. Delegation binds the formal organization together. It establishes superior–subordinate relationship and provides a basis for efficient functioning of the organization.
6. Delegation enables a manager to obtain the specialized knowledge and expertise of subordinates.
7. It helps to ensure continuity in business because managers of lower levels are enabled to acquire to valuable experienced in decision-making. They get an opportunity to develop their abilities and can fill higher positions in case of need.

3.8.6.6. Barriers to effective delegation

Many managers are found unwilling to delegate authority and many subordinates are found unwilling to accept it. The reasons for this unwillingness on both sides are as under:

(A) Manager's side:

- *Fear of loss of power:* Some managers are little Napoleans who want to keep all the authority to make decisions in their own hand. They feel uncomfortable when they see their subordinates making decisions, which they themselves once made.
- *I can do it better myself fallacy:* Some managers have an inflated sense of their own worth. They, therefore, want to perform themselves all jobs, which come their way.
- *Lack of confidence in subordinates:* Some managers hesitate to delegate authority to their subordinates because they doubt their ability. Such managers continue to keep themselves involved in jobs, which they have delegated to their subordinates.
- *Fear of being exposed:* Some inefficient managers are always afraid of their subordinates outshining them and providing more efficient. They are therefore, very cautious about delegating, lest their inefficiency be exposed.
- *Difficulty in briefing:* Many times managers are reluctant to delegate because they think that it is easier to do a task themselves than to brief the subordinates.

(B) Subordinate's side:

- They may refuse to accept authority because of their fear of criticism by their superior in case of commit mistakes in decision-making.
- They avoid accepting any authority if they feel that they lack adequate information and resources to help them discharge their duties properly.
- They may lack self-confidence and initiative and this may also be the cause for their unwillingness to accept any authority.
- They may avoid accepting any authority because there are no positive personal gains to them for assuming extra responsibility.

3.8.7. Decentralization of Authority

Centralization and decentralization refer to the location of decision-making authority in an organization. Centralization means that the authority for most decisions is concentrated at the top of the managerial hierarchy whereas decentralization requires such authority to be dispersed by extension and delegation through all levels of management. Actually these terms denote different degree of delegation of authority.

Louis A. Allen has defined both terms as "Centralization is the systematic and consistent reservation of authority at central points within an organization. Decentralization applies to the systematic delegation of authority in an organization–wide context."

Centralization and decentralization are opposite but relative terms because every organization contains both the features. There cannot be absolute centralization and absolute decentralization in practice. In case of having absolute centralization, each and every decision is to be taken by top-level management. But practically it is not possible; some decentralization exists in all organizations. In case of having absolute decentralization, there is no control over the activities of the subordinates, which is also not practicable. Therefore, effective decentralization of authority requires a proper balance between dispersal of authority among lower levels and adequate control over them.

3.8.7.1. Difference between Delegation and Decentralization

Sl.No.	Delegation	Decentralisation
1	It is process of devolution of authority.	It is the end result achieved by the delegation.
2	It implies the relationship between a superior and a subordinate.	It implies the relationship between top management and various departments and sections.
3	In delegation control rests entirely with the superior.	Here the top management exercises only overall control and delegates the authority for control to the departmental heads.
4	It is must for management.	It is optional.
5	It is a technique of management to get things done.	It is both technique and philosophy of management.
6	It can take place without decentralization.	There cannot be decentralization without delegation.

3.9 STAFFING

3.9.1. Meaning of Staffing

Staffing is an important function involved in building the human organization. ***In staffing, the manager attempts to find the right person for each job. Staffing fixes a manager's responsibility to***

recruit and to make certain that there is enough manpower available to fill the various positions needed in the organization. Staffing involves the selection and training of future managers and a suitable system of compensation. Staffing obviously cannot be done once and for all, since people are continually leaving, getting fired, retiring and dying. Often too, the changes in the organization create new positions, and these must be filled.

In other words, staffing is concerned with obtaining, utilizing and maintaining a satisfactory and satisfied work force. Its purpose is to establish and maintain sound personnel relations at all levels in the organization so as to make effective use of personnel to attain the objectives of the organization and to provide personal and social satisfaction, which personnel want. Staffing consists of wide range of interrelated activities.

Staffing is a very important function of management. No organization can be successful unless it can fill and keep filled the various positions with the right type of employees. Managers would be more competent and effective if they are carefully selected and trained. Staffing provides manpower, which is the key input of an organization.

Staffing function has the following sub functions. They are manpower planning, recruitment, selection, training and development, placement, compensation, promotion, appraisal etc.

3.9.2. Definition

"The managerial function of staffing involves manning the organizational structure through proper and effective selection, appraisal and development of personnel to fill the roles designed into the structure."

—Koontz and O'Donnell

"The process involved in identifying, assessing, placing, evaluating and directing individuals at work."

—S.Benjamin

3.9.3. Advantages of Staffing

1. It helps in discovering and obtaining competent personnel for various jobs.
2. It makes for higher performance by placing right persons on the right jobs.
3. It improves job satisfaction and morale of employees through objective assessment and fair compensation of their contributions.
4. It facilitates optimum utilization of human resources and in minimizing costs of manpower.
5. It ensures the continuity and growth of the organization through the development of managers.
6. It enables an organization to cope with the shortage of executive talent.

3.9.4. Need for Staffing

1. ***Increasing size of organization.*** In a large organization, there are several positions. Systematic programmes for the selection, training and appraisal of employees are required for efficient functioning of the enterprise. This has increased the significance of staffing.

2. ***Advancement of technology.*** Significant improvements have taken place in technology. In order to make use of the latest technology, the appointment of right type of persons is necessary. Right personnel can be procured, developed and maintained for new jobs only if the management performs its staffing function effectively.
3. ***Long-range needs for manpower.*** In order to execute the long-term plans, management must determine the manpower requirements well in advance. It is also necessary to develop managers for succession in future. The need for staffing has increased due to shortage of good managerial talent and high rate of labour turnover.
4. ***High wage bill.*** Personnel cost accounts for a major portions of operating costs today. Efficient performance of the staffing function is essential to make the best use of personnel. For example, if right type of people are selected and trained, management can obtain optimum results from the expenses incurred on recruitment, selection and training.
5. ***Trade unionism.*** Efficient system for staffing has become necessary to negotiate effectively with organizations of executives. With the spread of education, executives have become increasingly aware of their prerogatives. Collective bargaining has brought about change in their attitudes. Separation of ownership from management requires a more professional approach towards the staffing function.
6. ***Human relations movement.*** Enlightened employers have come to recognize the dignity of labour – increasing awareness of the role of human factor in industry. Now managers can use the knowledge of behavioural sciences in molding the behaviour of employees in the right direction. At the executive level, there is greater need for non-financial motivation. By performing the staffing function well, management can show the significance it attaches to the human resources in the organization.

3.9.5. Factors Affecting Staffing

Staffing is basically a dynamic process and is affected by a variety of factors both internal and external factors.

(A) External Factors

- *(i)* ***Political factors:*** Political stability, political parties and their political gimmicks, formation of new political parties, splits in trade unions etc. these changes in trade unions complicate the task of staffing.
- *(ii)* ***Economic factors:*** Number of economic factors affects staffing of an organization by influencing system, national income, per capita income, distribution of income and wealth etc.
- *(iii)* ***Social factors:*** Social environment consists of social roles, social values, caste structure, occupational structure, social forward and backward sections, religions, culture etc. These factors are also affect the staffing.
- *(iv)* ***Legal factors:*** There are various provisions, which affect the staffing policy of an organization. The act 1986, provide the restrictions of free recruitment of child labour. These factors also affect the staffing process of the organization.

(*v*) ***Customers:*** Any organization depends upon customers for their survival and growth. Organization's services are less qualitative in which customers may develop negative attitude towards the organization.

(B) Internal Factors

(*i*) ***Size of the organization:*** Staffing practices depends upon the size of the organization. A small organization cannot have the same staffing practices, which a large organization may have.

(*ii*) ***Organizational image:*** The image of an organization in human resource market depends on its staffing practices like facilities for training and development, compensation and incentives, and work culture. If all these factors are positive, an organization may be in a better position to attract the candidates and customers.

(*iii*) ***Technological factors:*** In technological changes technical personnel, skilled workers and machine operators are increasingly required while the demand for other employees has reduced. The procurement of skilled employees and their increase in numbers to match the changing job requirements has become a complicated task.

(*iv*) ***Changes in employee roles:*** Nowadays the relationship in which employees and management are partners in the organization, the management improves the staffing process by

- To provide various benefits to improve morale
- To introduce negotiating machinery to reduce grievances
- To encourage employee participation in decision-making.

(*v*) ***Education:*** In recent years increased formal education led to the changes in attitude of employees. The well-educated employees always challenge and question the management's decision and want a voice in the company's affairs affecting their interest. Thus management of well-educated employees is a problem to the organization though they make valuable contributions.

3.10. RECRUITMENT

3.10.1. Meaning

Recruitment is the process of identifying the sources of potential employees and encouraging them to apply for jobs in the organization. According to Dalton E. McFarland, "The term recruitment applies to the process of attracting potential employees to the company." The main purpose of recruitment is to create a pool of candidates from which personnel with required skills can be selected. Every organization has to recruit personnel through the amount of recruitment may differ from organization to organization depending upon the size of the organization, nature of job and the recruitment policy, etc.

3.10.2. Sources of Recruitment

The sources of recruitment can be broadly classified into two categories: internal and external. Internal sources refer to the present working force of a company. Selecting individuals from amongst the existing employees of the company may fill vacancies other than at the lowest level. Recruitment sources are two types. They are internal and external sources.

Internal Sources

- Present permanent employees
- Present temporary/casual employees
- Retired employees
- Dependents of deceased, disabled, retired and present employees.

Merits of Internal Sources

- Internal recruitment can be used as a technique of motivation
- Morale of the employees can be improved
- Employees economic needs for promotion, higher income can be satisfied
- Trade unions can be satisfied
- Employees become loyal to the enterprise
- Industrial peace is ensured
- People recruited from within the organization do not need induction training
- A better employee-employer relationship is established.

Demerits of Internal Sources

- It may encourage favouritism and nepotism
- This method limits the choice of selection to the few candidates available within the enterprise
- It may lead to inbreeding, resulting in promotion of people who have developed a respect for the tradition and who have no new ideas of their own. It is generally the new blood which brings in new ideas.

External Sources

- Re-employing former employees
- Friends and relatives of present employees
- Applicants at the gate
- College and technical institutions
- Employment exchanges
- Advertising agency
- Labour union

1. *Re-employing former employees:* Former employees who have been laid-off or have left for personal reasons may be re-employed. These people may require less initial training than that needed by total strangers to the enterprise.

2. ***Friends and relatives of present employees:*** Some industries with a record of good personnel relations encourage their employees to recommend their friends and relatives for appointment in the concern where they are employed.
3. ***Applicants at the gate:*** The factory representative interviews unemployed persons who call at the gates of the factories and those who are found suitable for the existing vacancies are selected. This is an important source in countries where there is a lot of unemployment.
4. ***College and technical institutions:*** Many big companies remain in touch with the colleges and technical institutions from where young and talented persons may be recruited. This type of source is more popular in advanced countries where there is a shortage of highly qualified technical people.
5. ***Employment exchanges:*** Employment exchanges also serve as an important source of recruitment for a number of business concerns. They are considered a useful source for the recruitment of clerks, accountants, typists, etc.
6. ***Advertising the vacancy:*** One more source that is tapped by the companies is advertising the vacancy in leading papers. This source may be used in case the company requires the services of persons possessing certain special skills or if there is an acute shortage of labour force.
7. ***Labour unions:*** In companies with strong labour unions, persons are sometimes recommended for appointment by their labour unions. This may also be done in pursuance to an agreement between the union and the management.

3.10.3. Selection

3.10.3.1. Meaning

Selection is the process of carefully screening the candidates who offer themselves for appointment so as to choose the most suitable persons for the jobs that are to be filled. It is the process of matching the qualifications of candidates with the requirements of jobs to be filled.

3.10.3.2. Selection Procedure

There can be no standard procedure to select different types of employees or to be adopted by all concerns. In practice, selection procedure differs from job to job and from organization to organization. In some cases, selection is a very simple and one-step process. But in many cases, it is quite complex and time-consuming.

The main steps in selection procedure may be as follows:

- Preliminary Interview
- Application blank
- Selection tests
- Employment interview
- Group discussion
- Checking of references

- Physical examination, and
- Final approval.

1. ***Preliminary interview.*** The purpose of preliminary interview is to eliminate the totally unsuitable candidates. It is generally brief and may take place across the counter in the employment office of the company. It consists of a short exchange of information regarding the candidate's age, qualifications, experience and interests. It helps to determine whether it is worthwhile for the candidate to fill in an application form. It saves the expense of processing unsuitable candidates and saves the candidate from the trouble of passing through the long procedure. Preliminary interview provides basic information about candidates.
2. ***Application blank.*** Candidates who get through the preliminary interview are asked to fill up a blank application form specially designed to obtain the required information about the candidate. Different types of application forms are used by different organizations and for different jobs. As far as possible, the application blank should be brief and simple. It should elicit only such information, which is relevant for the job concerned. Generally, an application form contains information regarding (a) personal history – name, date of birth, sex, marital status, nationality, etc. of the candidate, (b) educational qualifications, (c) job experience, and (d) references, etc.
3. ***Selection tests.*** Tests have become an important device in the process of selection. These are used to measure such skills and abilities, which are needed for efficient performance of the job. Several types of tests are used in practice for screening applicants. Written test may be descriptive or objective in nature.
4. ***Employment interview.*** Personal interview is perhaps the most widely used method for selecting employees. It is a face-to-face talk between the employer and the candidate. It is more thorough and comprehensive than the preliminary interview. The main purpose of employment interview are: (*a*) to check the information obtained in earlier steps, (*b*) to seek more information about the candidate, (*c*) to test the qualities of the candidate, and (*d*) to inform the candidate about the job and the organization. Personal and social traits like aptitude, interest, motivation, communicating skill, etc. can better be judged in an interview.
5. ***Checking reference.*** Candidates are usually required to provide some reference, i.e., names of persons to whom inquiries as to his educational background, experience, ability, character, etc., could be addressed. A reference can be a useful source of information in case lie is sufficiently knowledgeable and truthful. He may be the previous employer or teacher of the candidate. Before making final selection, the enterprise may contact the references to seek information on the candidate's ability and integrity. A letter of recommendation may also be asked from the candidate. Checking the references may help to point out discrepancies regarding the candidate's previous employment, past salary and reasons for leaving the job.
6. ***Group discussion.*** This method is being increasingly used for the selection of executives and civil servants. Under this method, several candidates are brought together and given a topic for discussion. Interviewers sit at the back and observe how each candidate

participates in the discussions. This method reveals personality characteristics, communication skills, ability to argue logically, ability to get on with others, ability to appreciate others' ideas, etc.

7. ***Physical examination.*** Physical or medical examination of a candidate is carried out to ascertain his physical fitness for the job. A proper medical examination will ensure high standards of health and physical fitness of the employees. It will reduce the rates of absenteeism, accidents and labour turnover. A thorough medical check of candidates fulfills three objectives:
   - First, it helps to ascertain the applicant's physical capability to meet the job requirement.
   - Secondly, it helps to prevent communicable diseases entering the organization.
   - Thirdly, it protects the organization against unwarranted claims under the Workmen's Compensation Act.
8. ***Final approval.*** After screening the candidates a list of suitable candidates is prepared. The list is sent to the line manager who requisitioned the personnel. He gives the final approval. The candidates formally approved by the manager concerned are appointed by issuing appointment letters and concluding service agreements.

3.11. TRAINING AND DEVELOPMENT

3.11.1. Meaning

Training is an organized process for increasing the knowledge and skills of the people for doing a particular job. It is a learning process involving the acquisition of skills and attitude. The purpose of training is to improve the current performance. Training is a continuous process because a person never stops training. Training should be differentiated from education development.

3.11.2. Training Methods

The various methods of training and developing executives may be classified as follows:

1. *On-The-Job Methods*
   - Experience
   - Coaching
   - Under study
   - Position rotation
   - Special projects and task forces
   - Committee assignments
   - Multiple managements

2. *Off-The-Job Methods*
- Selected readings
- Conferences and seminars
- Special courses
- Case Study
- Programmed Instruction
- Brain storming
- In-Basket exercise
- Role playing
- Management games
- Sensitivity training

1. ***On-the-Job Training.*** On the job training involves by doing. It is considered to be an effective approach for making managers more competent. The trainee is motivated to learn because the training takes place in the real job situation. Little additional space and equipment is needed for training. But neither the trainee nor the trainers are free from the daily pressure of job. The trainer has seldom the time and patience to impart effective training.

(i) ***Experience:*** This is one of the oldest methods of on-the-job training. It involves learning by doing. It is the most practical and effective method. But it is wasteful and inefficient.

(ii) ***Coaching and counseling:*** Under this method, the senior or superior plays the role of the guide and instructor of the management trainee. He provides personal instruction and guidance. He demonstrates the task operations and answers queries. The trainee observes the superior carefully to learn the necessary skills of the functional area. He mentally visualizes and rehearses different facts of the job. Coaching is one of the oldest and the vest methods of developing managers on the job. Training rakes place in a realistic environment and the trainee is motivated to learn. The senior is in the best position to monitor and develop managerial qualities in the subordinate. But the stress and strain of the daily duties do not permit complete concentration on training. The senior seldom finds enough time and attention for providing training. He may not be properly trained and oriented himself.

(iii) ***Under study or attachment method:*** When a person is promoted to higher level he is given training in the job to which he is to be appointed. He is chosen as the successor to the current incumbent who is going to retire or resign. The trainee is attached with the senior and is called an understudy assistant to apprentice. He is given adequate authority to take decision. He is not penalized for the mistakes committed during the course of learning.

(iv) ***Position rotation:*** Position rotation is the process of training executives by rotating them through a series of related jobs or positions. The trainee learns several different jobs within a work unit or department. He performs each job for a specified and limited period. Some companies follow the channel method under which a particular discipline is earmarked for progression of the junior manager.

(v) ***Special project and task forces:*** Under this method the trainee is assigned a project closely related to his job. For example, management trainees in accounts may be asked to develop a cost control system. The trainee learn by performing the special assignment not only work procedures but organizational relationships too. Sometimes a task force is created consisting of executives from different functional areas. The trainee learns how to work with others.

(vi) ***Committee assignments:*** Under this methods the trainee managers are appointed as members of a committee. The committee deliberates upon and discusses problem of enterprises. By participating in meetings and discussions, every member learns analytical thinking and decision making skills, managers keep abreast of current devilments either respective areas of specialization. Committees provide an opportunity to know what is happening in the rest of the organization.

(vii) ***Junior boards or multiple management:*** This technique was developed by Carles Mc Cormick of Baltimore, USA under it a junior board of executives is constituted. In this board executives discuss real life problems debate different viewpoints and take decisions, the participants learn comprehension analysis and decision-making.

2. ***Off the Job Training.*** In recent years formal training and management development programmers have become very popular due to the limitations of on the job training does not provide adequate expertise environment and facilities. Secondly on the job training is inadequate for developing improved behaviour patterns in managers. Thirdly highly sophisticated tasks and techniques of management development are now available. Training has become a specialized job. Fourthly effective training requires a great deal of participation and group discussion among participants from diverse disciplines and cultures. This is not always possible in case of on the job training. Fifthly, a behaviour modification of trainees requires a simulated and highly maneuvered atmosphere not found in on the job training. In on the job training, trainees are under the pressure and inhabitations of the daily work routine. Of the job training provides an uninhibited and relaxed environment. The main drawback in off the job training is the artificial work environment, which requires adjustment to the actual work situations after the training.

(i) ***Selected readings:*** This a self-improvement programme under which executives acquire knowledge by reading professional journals and advanced books on management. Many organizations maintain their own libraries of this purpose. Moreover, executives may become members of the professional associations to keep abreast of latest developments in management.

(ii) ***Conferences and seminars:*** In a conference, participants are required to pool their ideas viewpoints and suggestions. The participants are normally drawn from different companies and sectors. Sometimes a conference is divided into small groups. These groups discuss thoroughly the problems of common interest and report their recommendations to the conference. Conferences provided a common platform for intensive group discussion and allow the participants to look at the problem from different angles.

(iii) ***Special courses and lectures:*** Special courses are designed by the company itself or by management schools. Companies sponsor their executives to attend these courses.

The participants are given classroom instructions through lectures and audiovisual aids; they are imparted concepts, principles and techniques in various areas of managements. For example, General management, finance and accounts, marketing, production, personnel, and industrial relations.

(iv) ***Case study method:*** A case is typically a record of an actual business issue, which has been faced by business executives together with surroundings, facts, opinions and prejudices upon which executive decision had to depend. The case is presented to the trainee for discussion and analysis. The trainee are excepted to identify and diagnose the problem involved, generate alternative courses of an action analyze the pros and cons of each alternative and arrive at recommendation which the managements should adopt under the given circumstances.

(v) ***Programmed instruction:*** It is a technique of instruction without the intervention of a human instructor. It is a learner-centered method wherein the subject matter is presented to the trainees in small steps and they are asked to make frequent responses. They are given feedback on their responses the information is broken into meaningful units and rearranged into a proper machines sequence so as to form learning package manuals, electronic teaching machines and computer systems are useful method for building knowledge and for retention of that knowledge.

(vi) ***Brain storming:*** Under this method a problem is put before a group of trainees and they are encouraged to offer ideas or suggestions. Criticism of any idea is not allowed so as to reduce inhibiting forces. Each trainee is allowed maximum possible participations later on all the ideas are critically examined the purpose is to maximize innovation and creativity on the part of executives.

(vii) ***In Basket exercise:*** In the basket contains a number of correspondences, each of which poses a problem. The problem is of different kinds and resembles real life problems. The trainees study memos, letters, reports, and other documents in the basket. They are required to solve each problem and to record their decisions within a specified time period. The participants learn logical thinking; inter relationship between problems and decision-making skills.

(viii) ***Role playing:*** Under this method two or more trainees spontaneously act out or play role in artificially created situations. They act out the given roles, as they would be playing in real life situations. They are informed of the roles, as they would be playing in real life situation. They are informed of the situation and the roles they are expected to play.

(ix) ***Management games:*** Under this method, an actual business situation is presented as a model. The participants compete with each other to analyze the problem and to take decisions; their decisions are processed in stages. A performance report is prepared periodically to measure the success of the participants. This method is useful in developing the ability of taking decisions with incomplete data and amid conditions of uncertainty. It improves power of anticipation and prediction of the competitor's action.

(x) ***Sensitivity training:*** Under this method, a small group meets in an unstructured situation. There is no plan or schedule and no agenda or other inhibitions. The numbers of the groups are allowed to communicate with each other freely so that each can gain an insight of his behavior as others see. The trainees are encouraged to probe their feelings and abilities and building inter personal relationships.

3.12. PERFORMANCE APPRAISAL

3.12.1. Meaning

Performance appraisal or merit rating is one of the oldest and most universal practices of managements. It refers to all the formal procedures used in working organizations to evaluate the personalities and contributions and potential of group members.

3.12.2. Criteria for Performance Appraisal

There are a number of performance criteria, which may be used to measure the proficiency of an employee. These criteria may be classified into two main categories: objective criteria and subjective criteria. Amount of quality of production, work sample tests, length of service, amount of training necessary, absenteeism, accidents etc., are all examples of objective criteria ratings of employees job proficiency by their superiors, peers and subordinates, extent of upward communication of ideas, degree of knowledge about corporate goals, contribution to socio cultural values etc., are examples of subjective criteria. Since all subjective criteria depend upon human judgment and opinion, they are subject to certain kinds of errors likely to be found in rating process.

3.12.3. Methods of Performance Appraisal

The various methods of performance appraisal may broadly be classified into two categories:

(*i*) Trait-based appraisal, and (*ii*) Appraisal by results.

(i) Trait-based methods of appraisal. Traditionally, managers have been evaluated against standards of personal traits and work characteristics. The traits (qualities) generally considered are as follows:

(*a*) Job knowledge,

(*b*) Ability to get along with people

(*c*) Analytical competence

(*d*) Leadership

(*e*) Judgement, and

(*f*) Initiative

The main methods of performance appraisal based on the traits of employees are given below.

1. ***Ranking Method:*** Under this method an employee is compared with all other employees in the group and placed in a simple rank order. In this way all individuals are rated from the best to the worst. This method is very simple and natural. It is the oldest method. But

it suffers from several limitations. First, the method is highly subjective. Secondly, it does not evaluate individual traits and only the personality of the whole man is evaluated. Thirdly, degree of difference in ability between ranks is not measured. Fourthly, in a large group the rater finds it very difficult to compare several people simultaneously. This method is useful if the number of employee is very small.

2. ***Paired Comparison Method:*** This is a variation of the ranking method. In this method, the rater compares each individual in the group with every other individual. The final ranking of each worker is determined by the number of times he was judged better than the others. The number of pairs (comparisons) to be made can be determined by the following formula:

$$\text{Number of pairs} = N\,(N-1)/2$$

where N stands for the number of person to be rated. This is an improvement over the ranking method. One limitation of this approach is that the number of comparisons becomes very large. For example, in a group of 50 workers, there would be 1,225 comparisons.

3. ***Graphic Rating Scales:*** A graphic scale is a chart that presents the list of qualities and the range of degree for each quality. Numerical values are assigned to each quality on the scale. The scales used are generally of two types viz., discrete scales and continuous scales.

(*a*) **Discrete scales:** In which two or more categories representing discrete degrees of ability are given. For example, the trait 'job knowledge' may be divided into five categories, as shown below

Poor	Below Average	Average	Above average	Outstanding

(*b*) **Continuous scales:** Wherein an uninterrupted lines is given and the rater can tick at any point along its length as shown below:

1,2	3	4,5	6,7	8,9,10
Poor	Below Average	Average	Above Average	Exceptionally Good

The basic idea behind this type of scale is to provide the rater with a continuum representing varying degrees of a particular trait.

Graphic rating scales are widely used for rating employees. These scales provide information on the size of differences in ratings and help to overcome the problem of a larger number of ratings. It is easy to construct and administer the scales. But there is a tendency on the part of the raters to pile up the ratings either at the middle or at the higher end of the scale. There may be differences in interpretation among different raters and as a result the ratings by different raters might not be comparable. Statements describing the actual behaviour of people e.g., 'unfamiliar with work', 'fairly familiar with work' and 'thoroughly familiar with work' convey a better meaning than adjectives like 'poor', 'below average', etc.

4. ***Forced Distribution Method:*** Under this method certain categories (grades) of ability are established and certain percentage of marks are assigned for each grade. The rater is

forced to distribute the ratings fairly among different grades. Example, poor 10% Below average 20%, Average 40% Above average 20% and Outstanding 10%. The employee is assigned the grade which best represents his caliber. This method overcomes the limitation of piling up of rating on one side of the scale. It minimizes the bias of the rater. But employees are rated for overall performance and not for individual traits.

5. ***Forced Choice Description:*** In this method, a number of statements describing the employees are prepared and the rater is forced to choose among the descriptive statements. The statements may be both favourable and unfavourable. The rater ticks two statements, one most characteristic and the other least characteristic of the person being rated. For example, a forced choice block may be as follows:

   (*i*) He is hard working

   (*ii*) He is not dependable

   (*iii*) He gives clear instructions

   (*iv*) He shows favouritism towards some employees.

6. ***Checklist Method:*** A checklist is a list of statements that describe the worker and his behaviour. Each statement is assigned a weight or value depending upon its importance. The rater writes 'yes' or ' no' against each statement depending upon whether it is applicable to the worker being rated or not. An individual's rating is determined by adding together the weights of statements applicable to the individual. A specimen checklist is given below:

(*i*) He is punctual	Yes/No
(*ii*) He has thorough knowledge of the job	Yes/No
(*iii*) He can easily locate faults	Yes/No
(*iv*) He does not discriminate among employees	Yes/No

7. ***Critical Incidents Method:*** Under this method certain key factors that make the difference between success and failure are identified. These critical incidents are converted into scales. The superior then observes and records instances and events of on-the-job behaviour falling under any of the identified factors. In this way a concrete performance record based on actual happenings is obtained. For example, the critical incidents in the career of an employee may be as follows:

   (*i*) Suggested improvement in work method,

   (*ii*) Refused to obey orders

   (*iii*) Violated the established rule, and

   (*iv*) Averted a serious accident.

(ii) Appraisal by Results: Trait-based appraisal is simple and economical. But it is not very reliable because of the subjectivity and bias on the part of raters. Executives dislike being evaluated by traits rather than on their accomplishments. Managers feel that performance is in itself the most reliable indicator of quality and potential. This feeling has led to the growth of appraisal by results. The method under plays traits and other characteristics, focusing on performance results. The process of result-oriented appraisal consists of the following steps:

1. The superior and each of his subordinates jointly establish the subordinate's tasks and responsibilities.
2. The subordinate prepares a plan for a specified period, e.g., six months or one year.
3. Through mutual consultation, the final target to be achieved by the subordinate and superior's supporting role are fixed.
4. At the end of the specified period, the superior makes an appraisal of the subordinate on the basis of mutually agreed criteria.
5. Superior discusses the results and his evaluation with the subordinate. Corrective actions, if necessary, are suggested and mutually agreed upon targets are fixed for future.

360° Performance Appraisal

The appraiser may be any person who has thorough knowledge about the job content, contents to be appraised, standards of contents and who observes the employee while performing a job. The appraiser should be capable of determining what is more important and what is relatively less important. He should prepare reports and make judgments without bias.

Typical appraisers are:

- Supervisors
- Peers
- Subordinates
- Employees themselves
- Users of service and
- Consultants.

Performance appraisal by all these parties is called "360° Performance Appraisal." Pond's, General Electric, Hindustan Lever Limited, Grasim, Colgate-Palmolive, Hewlett-Packard, companies adopted 360° performance appraisal.

1. **Supervisors.** Supervisors include superiors of the employee, other superiors having knowledge about the work of the employee and department head or manager. General practice is that immediate superiors appraise the performance which in turn is reviewed by the departmental head/manager.
2. **Peers.** Peer appraisal may be reliable if the work group is stable over a reasonably long period of time and performs tasks that require interaction. However, little research has been conducted to determine how peers establish standards for evaluating others or the overall effect of peer appraisal on the group's attitude.
3. **Subordinates.** The concept of having superiors rated by subordinates is being used in most organizations today, especially in developed countries. Such a novel method can be useful in other organizational settings too provided the relationships between superiors and subordinates are cordial.
4. **Self Appraisal.** If individuals understand the objectives they are expected to achieve and the standards by which they are to be evaluated, they are to a great extent in the best position to appraise their own performance. Also, since employee development means

self development, employees who appraise their own performance may become highly motivated. Thermax, Escorts, Wipro etc. implement self appraisal.

5. **Users of Services/Customers.** Employee performance in service organizations relating to behaviours, promptness, speed in doing the job and accuracy can be better judged by the customers or users of services.

   For example, teacher's performance is better judged by students and the performance of a doctor is judged by the patients.

6. **Consultants.** Sometimes consultants may be engaged for appraisal when employees or employers do not trust supervisor appraisal and the management does not trust self-appraisal, peer appraisal or subordinate appraisal. In this situation, consultants are trained and they observe the employee at work for a sufficiently long time for the purpose of appraisal.

When to Appraise?

Informal appraisals are conducted whenever the supervisor or personnel managers feel it necessary. However, systematic appraisals are conducted on a regular basis, say for example, every six months or annually.

Chapter 4 LEADERSHIP

4.1. LEADERSHIP

Leadership is a term that conjures up different images in different people. While to some it means charisma, to others, it means power and authority.

4.1.1. Definition

> ***"Leadership is the activity of influencing people to strive willingly for group objectives".***
>
> —*George K. Terry*
>
> ***"Leader as the art or process of influencing people so that they will strive willingly and enthusiastically towards the achievement of group goals".***
>
> ***"Leadership is the quality of behaviour of individuals whereby they guide people or their activities in organizing efforts".***
>
> —*Koontz et. al.*

After going through the above definitions of leadership, it can safely be defined as a process of influencing group activities towards the achievement of certain goals.

The person who guides or influences the behaviour of others called 'leader' and people guided or influenced are called the 'followers'.

4.1.2. Characteristics of leadership

1. Leadership is a continuous process of influencing other's behaviour.
2. Leadership basically a personal quality that enable leader to influence the subordinate's behaviour at work.

3. The success of a leader depends on the acceptance of his leadership by the followers. Of course, the situational variables also affect the effectiveness of leadership.
4. There is a relationship between leader and followers, which arises out of functioning for a common goal.

4.1.3. Ingredients of Leadership

Leaders envision the future; they inspire organization members and chart the course of the organization. Every group of people that performs near its total capacity has some person as its head who is skilled in the art of leadership. This skill seems to be a compound of at least four major ingredients.

- *The ability to use power effectively and in a responsible manner.*
- *The ability to comprehend that human beings have different motivation forces at different times and in different situations.*
- *The ability to inspire and ,*
- *The ability of act in a manner that will develop a climate conducive to responding to and arousing motivations.*

4.1.4. Leadership Styles

There are three basic styles of leadership:

- Autocratic or Authoritative Style
- Democratic or Participative Style
- Laissez-Faire or Free-Rein Style

(a) ***Autocratic or Authoritative Style.*** In autocratic style, the leader centralizes power and decision-making in himself/herself. The leader commands complete control over the subordinates who are compelled to obey the orders. The subordinates have no opportunity to make suggestions or take part in decision-making function. The autocratic leader has little concern for the well being of employees. In turn, employees have a tendency to avoid responsibility and try to work as little as possible. They also suffer from frustration and low morale.

Limitations of autocratic leadership style

- It results in low morale and job satisfaction.
- Employee's efficiency tends to decline over period.
- Potential manager-leader employees do not get opportunity to exhibit their capabilities.

However, the autocratic style of leadership is suitable in the following situations when:

- Subordinates are incompetent and inexperienced.
- The leader wants to be active and dominant in decision-making.
- The leader is highly competent for making a right decision.

(b) Democratic or Participative Style. In democratic style of leadership, the leader takes decision in consultation with the subordinates. In other words, the subordinates participate in decision-making function. Hence, the style is also known as Participative style. Participation in decision-making enables subordinate to satisfy their social and ego needs. It also makes them more committed to their organizations. Frequent interaction between the manager-leader and subordinates also helps build up mutual faith and confidence.

Advantages

1. It gives opportunity to the subordinates to develop their potential abilities and assume greater responsibilities.
2. It provides job satisfaction, on the one hand, and improves the morale of subordinates, on the other.
3. Subordinates' participation in decision-making helps make right decision because 'two heads are better than one'.

Despite the above benefits, democratic style leadership cannot be regarded as the best style under all situations.

Limitations

- Decision-making is a time-consuming process in democratic style.
- There is possibility that a few dominant subordinates may influence decision in their favour.
- The responsibility for implementing decision cannot be fixed on an individual subordinate but on the whole group.
- Sometimes the decisions taken become the distorted one because 'Many cooks spoil the broth'.

However, the democratic style is found suitable in the following situations when:

1. Subordinates are competent and experienced.
2. The leader prefers participative decision-making.
3. The organization has made its objectives transparent to the employees.
4. Reward and involvement are used as the primary means of motivation and control.

(c) Laissez-Faire Style (or) Free-Rein Style. Laissez faire style is just the opposite of autocratic style. In Laissez-faire style, the manager-leader leaves decision-making to the subordinates. The leader completely gives up his/her leadership role. The subordinates enjoy full freedom to decide as and what they like. The biggest limitation of this style is that due to full freedom to subordinates, it creates chaos and mismanagement in decision-making.

Nonetheless, laissez faire style is found suitable in the following situations when:

- *Leader is able to fully delegate the powers of decision-making to his/her subordinates.*
- *Subordinates are also well competent and knowledgeable.*
- *Organizational goals and objectives*

4.1.5. Leadership Theories

There are a number of theories, which provide explanations regarding various aspects of leadership phenomenon. Some of the important theories are discussed below:

4.1.5.1. Fiedler's Contingency Model

According to the contingency theories of leadership, the success of leadership depends upon the situation in which the leader operates. Fred E. Fiedler developed a contingency model of leadership. According to him, a leader's effectiveness depends upon the following three situational factors:

- *Leader-followers relations, that is the degree of follower's trust confidence and respect for the leader.*
- *Task Structure, that is the nature of task performed by the subordinates.*
- *The Status Power, that is the degree of power associated with the position or status held by the leader in the organization.*

The most favourable situation for leaders to influence their group is one in which they are well liked by the members, the task performed is highly structured and the leader has enough power attached to his/her position in the organization. On the other hand, the most unfavourable situation for leaders is one in which they are disliked, the task is highly unstructured and little power is attached to the leader's position.

4.1.5.2. Path-goal Leadership Theory

Robert House has developed a path-goal theory of leadership initially presented by Martin Evans. This theory is based on the expectancy theory of motivation. The theory states that leaders can exercise four different kinds of styles. Directive leadership (giving directions to the subordinates rather than seeking their cooperation). Supportive leadership (being friendly and approachable to subordinates), participative leadership (asking for suggestions from subordinates before making decisions.) and achievement-oriented leadership (setting challenging goals and assignments for subordinates). The path-goal theory postulates that leaders become effective due to their influence on followers' motivation, ability to perform, and their satisfaction. Leader motivates the employees by influencing their expectancies relating to the performance and attractiveness of goal. The subordinates feel satisfied when they believe that their job performance will lead to desirable outcomes. They will be able to achieve their goals with hard work.

4.1.5.3. Situational Leadership Theory

The situational leadership model is developed by Paul Hersey and Kenneth Blanchard, which suggests that the leadership effectiveness depends upon the situation in which leadership is exercised. In their model, the authors have employed two dimensions of leader behaviour as were used in Ohio State University studies as discussed earlier. The two dimensions were task (production-oriented) and relationship (people-oriented). The level of followers' development, or say, maturity is categorized into four levels based on their ability and willingness to accept responsibility for completing their task. Followers who are unable and unwilling are categorized as the least nature, and those who are both able and willing are termed as the most mature. The model suggests that the two different types of styles are used to influence the followers of four different levels of maturity as is depicted in the following figure.

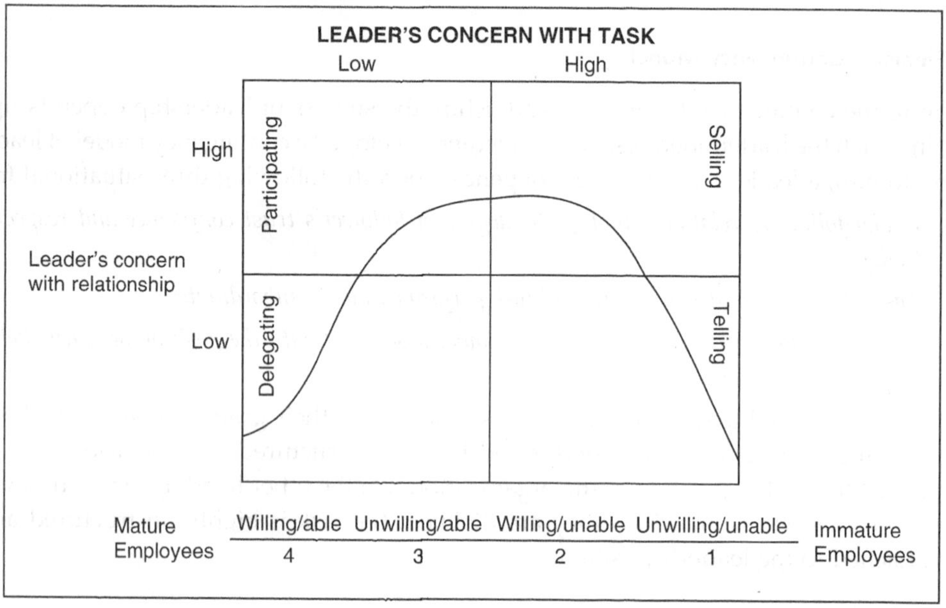

The Hersey-Blanchard Model of the Situational Leadership Model

It is seen from the above Figure that the leadership style varies across the levels of followers' maturity. A leader needs to use a telling style of leadership with immature followers who are not unable and unwilling to take responsibility for completing their work. Once the followers mature to the second level, the leader needs to exercise a selling style. Followers further matured i.e., able but unwilling, need to be led by employing participating style by the leader. Finally, the most mature followers who are able as well as willing require to be led by a delegating style of leadership for the simple reason because the followers accept responsibility entrusted upon them.

What leadership style should be employed at which maturity level of followers is now tabulated as follows:

TABLE. Followers' Maturity Level vis-à-vis Leadership Style

Maturity Level	Recommended Leadership Style
1. Low ability, low willingness	Telling (directive, low support)
2. Low ability, high willingness	Selling/coaching (directive, supportive)
3. High ability, low willingness	Participating/Supporting (Supportive/low direction)
4. High ability, high willingness	Delegating (low direction, low support)

However, one key limitation of the situational leadership model is the absence of central hypotheses that could be tested. It also does not have a widely accepted research base, which would make it a more valid and reliable theory of leadership. Nonetheless, the theory has intuitive appeal and is widely used for training and development in corporations. It has achieved considerable popularity and also awakened many managers to the idea of situational approaches to leadership styles.

4.1.5.4. The Managerial Grid

One of the most widely known styles of leadership is the managerial grid developed by Blake and Mouton. The grid is based on two underlying dimensions labeled as Concern for Production and Concern for people. Based on these two dimensions, the authors have generated a 9 by 9 grid representing concern for production along the horizontal dimension and concern for people along the vertical dimension. The authors have identified the five distinct managerial styles as shown in the following figure.

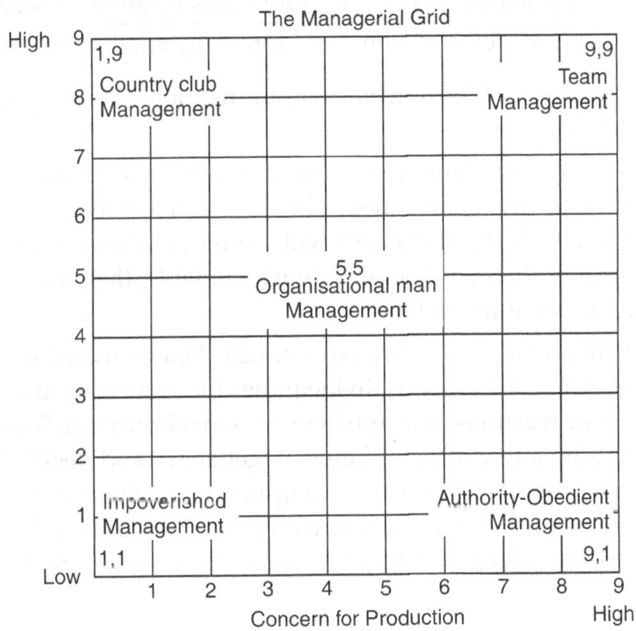

A brief description of these five leadership styles follows:

The impoverished manager (1.1) has low concern for both production and people. He exerts the minimum efforts to get essential work done, while maintaining organizational membership. This style of management is similar to the laissez-faire style as discussed earlier.

The country-club manager (1.9) has high concern for people but low concern for production. Good feelings towards followers are the hallmarks of such manager.

The authority-obedient manager (9.1) has more concern for production but low concern for people. Production maximization is the hallmark of such manager. This style is similar to the autocratic style of leadership.

The team-manager (9.9) has high concern for both production and people.

The organization man manager (5.5.) has moderate levels of concern for both production and people. Such manager goes along to get along, conforming to and maintaining the status quo.

The best style for all managers, in all organizations, and under all situations is the (9.9) team manager style.

4.1.5.5. Equity Theory

An important factor in motivation is whether individuals perceive the reward structure as being fair. One way of addressing this issue is through equity theory, which refers to an individual's subjective judgements about the fairness of the reward she or he got, relative to the inputs (which include many factors such as effort, experience, education, and so on), in comparison with the rewards of other. J. Stacy Adams has received a great deal of credit for the formulation of the equity (or inequity) theory. The essential aspects of the equity theory may be shown as follows.

$$\frac{\text{Outcomes by a person}}{\text{Inputs by a person}} = \frac{\text{Outcomes by another person}}{\text{Inputs by another person}}$$

There should be a balance of the outcomes-inputs relationship for one person in comparison with that for another person.

If people feel they are inequitably rewarded, they may be dissatisfied, reduce the quantity or quality of output, or leave the organization. They also can ask for a greater reward. If people perceive the rewards as equitable, they probably will continue at the same level of output. If people think the rewards are greater than what is considered equitable, they may work harder. It is also possible that some may discount the reward.

One of the problems is that people may overestimate their own contributions and the rewards others receive. Employees may tolerate certain inequities for some time. But prolonged feelings of inequity may result in strong reactions to an apparently minor occurrence. For example, an employee being reprimanded for being a few minutes late may get angry and decide to quit the job, not so much because of the reprimand but because of longstanding feelings that the rewards for his or her contributions are inequitable in comparison with others' rewards. Likewise a person may be very satisfied with a weekly salary of $500 until he or she finds out that another person doing similar work gets $10 more.

4.1.5.6. Reinforcement Theory

Psychologist B.E. Skinner of Harvard developed an interesting-but controversial-technique for motivation. The approach, called positive reinforcement or behaviour modification, holds that individuals can be motivated by proper design of their work environment and praise for their performance and that punishment for poor performance produces negative results.

Skinner and his followers do far more than praise good performance. They analyze the work situation to determine what causes workers to act the way they do, and then they initiate changes to eliminate troublesome areas and obstructions to performance. Specific goals are then set with workers' participation and assistance, prompt and regular feedback of results is made available, and performance improvements are rewarded with recognition and praise. Even when performance does not equal goals, ways are found to help people and praise them for the good things they do. It has also been found highly useful and motivating to give people full information on a company's problems, especially those in which they are involved.

This technique sounds almost too simple to work, and many behavioural scientists and managers are skeptical about its effectiveness. However, a number of prominent companies have found the approach beneficial. Emery Air Freight Corporation, for example, observed, that this approach saved the company a substantial amount of money by merely inducing employees to take great pains to ensure that containers were properly filled with small packages before shipment.

Perhaps the strength of the Skinner approach is that it is so closely akin to the requirements of good managing. It emphasizes removal of obstructions to performance, careful planning and organizing, control through feedback, and the expansion of communication.

4.2. MOTIVATION

4.2.1. Meaning

The term motivation has been derived from the word motive. Motive is anything that initiates or sustains activity. It is an inner state that energizes, activates or moves and that directs or channels behavior towards goals motive is a psychological force within an individual that sets him in motion.

4.2.2. Definition

"Motivation is a general term applying to the entire class of drives, desires, needs, wishes and similar forces that induce an individual or a group of people to work".

—Koontz & O'Donnell

"Motivation means a process of stimulating people to action to accomplish desired goals".

—Scott

4.2.3. Nature/Characteristics of Motivation

Following are the characteristics of motivations:

Motivation is a personal and internal feeling

Motivation is a psychological phenomenon, which generates within an individual. Motives are the energetic forces within a person that drive him to action.

Motivation produces goals directed behaviour

Motivation is a behavioural concept that directs human behaviour towards certain goals.

Motivation is a continuous process

Human needs are unlimited. Therefore, motivation is an ongoing process.

Motivation is complex

Individuals differ in their motivation. Different people seek different things or they work for different reasons. Human needs and motives are varies and they change form time to time. Human motivation is partly logical and partly emotional.

Motivation is system oriented

Motivation is the result of interplay among three groups of factors *(a) influences operating within an individual*, (for example, his goals needs and values). *(b) Influences operating within the organization*, (e.g. organization structure, technology, physical facilities and nature of the job, etc.,) and (c)*forces operating in the external environment*, (e.g. culture, customs, norms etc., of the society).

Motivation can be either positive or negative

Positive motivations implies use of pay incentives, etc., to satisfy human needs while negative motivation emphasizes penalties, e.g. reprimands, threats of demotion, fear or loss of job, etc.

Motivation is different from job satisfaction

Motivation is the drive to satisfy a want and it is concerned with goal directed behaviour. Satisfaction refers to contentment after the satisfaction of want. Motivation is the process while satisfaction is the outcome or consequence.

4.2.4. Importance of Motivation

A lot of importance has been given to the process of motivation in the area of organizational behaviour. The process of motivation is applicable to all cadres of employees, workers, supervisors, managers and employees in all walks of life.

The demotivated worker, demotivate others in the society and they cause much damage at home and in industries. Motivation is the basic factor and the cause for any behaviour. Motivation is only overt but also covert in nature. So, the expert in organization behaviour recognizes the importance of motivation and accords top priority to the concept.

Nowadays, managers spent more time in their attempts to motivate their subordinates than in any other managerial function. Yet the word motivation is often misused and misunderstood by many of us. It is the force or urge that is within the individuals that force them to act.

4.2.5. Motivational Techniques or Tools

Motivational tools or techniques are instruments that prompt people to action. Hence, while using motivational tools, these should be adequate and capable enough to motivate employees to make their maximum efforts to accomplish the set goals. Various motivational techniques are used to motivate employees in business organization are broadly classified into monetary (financial) and non-monetary (Non-financial) techniques of incentives.

As human needs vary between people and between different points of times in case the same person, motivational techniques are therefore bound to vary accordingly, for example, while increase in salary may satisfy one's physiological needs, recognition may satisfy the esteem needs. Better the motivational techniques, greater would be its effect on the individual behaviour. This would in turn lead to organizational effectiveness.

(I) Financial Incentives. Incentives, which are given in the form of money, are called financial incentives. This can be classified into two points.

- Individual financial incentives
- Collective financial incentives

(*a*) ***Individual financial incentives.*** This type of incentives includes all such incentive plans, which induce an individual to achieve higher output to earn higher financial reward. F.W.Taylor's piece rate system, Habey's efficiency plan are examples of such incentives. The basic assumptions behind these incentives are that an individual will be motivated for higher output to earn money, which satisfies his need.

(*b*) ***Collective financial incentives.*** This type of incentives tries to motivate individuals collectively. The basic ideas of these incentives are the same as the individual incentives. However, these incentives are collectively given to employees for motivating them, e.g., Bonus, profit sharing, Pension plan etc.

(II) Non-financial Incentives. Individuals have various needs, which want to satisfy while working in the organization. People at comparatively higher level of managerial hierarchy attach more importance to sociophychological needs, which can not be satisfied by money alone. Thus, management in addition to financial incentives, provide non-financial incentives to motivate people in the organization. The importance of non-financial incentive is to provide psychological and emotional satisfaction rather than financial satisfaction. For example, if an individual gets promotion in the organization, it satisfies him psychologically more i.e. he get better status, challenging job, authority etc. than financial benefits.

The non-financial incentives can be grouped as under:

- Individual non-financial incentives.
- Collective non-financial incentives.
- Institutional non-financial incentives.

(*a*) ***Individual non-financial incentives.*** These incentives motivate people on individual basis. The various forms of individual non-financial incentives are as follows:

- ***Status.*** Status means the ranking of position, rights and duties in the formal organization structure. It is an instrument of motivation because it is extremely required for most of the people. The status system should be closely related to the abilities and aspiration of people in the organization.
- ***Promotion.*** It is a movement to a higher position in which the responsibilities and powers are more. Promotion satisfies the needs of human beings in organization.
- ***Responsibility.*** Most of the people prefer challenging jobs or the jobs which has got more responsibilities rather than monotonous and routine in nature. If the job is connected with more responsibilities, it satisfies people's natural and inherent characters and they put more efforts in the respective jobs.
- ***Making the job pleasant and interesting.*** The work can be made enjoyable and pleasant if it so designed that it allows employees to satisfy the natural instincts. This create interest in the work and employees take it natural as play.

- ***Recognition of work.*** It means acknowledgement with a show of appreciation. When such appreciation is given to the work performed by the employees they feel motivated to perform work at similar (or) higher level.

(*b*) ***Collective non-financial incentives.*** Workers may be motivated in groups also. They perform their duties in groups and the group affects them. Some of the collective non-financial incentives are as follows:

- Social importance to work
- Team spirit
- Competition
- ***Social importance to work.*** People generally prefer a work, which is socially acceptable, if the society gives the importance and praise the work, people like to perform.
- ***Team spirit.*** Management should encourage Team spirit *i.e.,* work in co-operation and co-ordination.
- ***Competition.*** Sometimes for providing incentives to employees, competitions are organized between different individuals (or) different groups.

(*c*) ***Institutional non-financial incentives***

- ***Human Relations in industries.*** It is related with the policies to be adopted in the organization to develop a sense of belongingness with employees, improve the efficiency and treat them as human beings and not merely a factor of production.
- ***Participation.*** Participation is related to superior-subordinates, both involved in making decision and discharge their responsibilities towards achieving organizational objectives.

4.2.6. Theories of Motivation

When the human organizations were established, various thinkers have tried to find out the answer to what motivates people to work. Different approaches applied by them have resulted in a number of theories on motivation.

4.2.6.1. Maslow's Need Hierarchy Theory

Maslow's theory is based on the human needs. Drawing chiefly on his clinical experience, he classified all human needs into a hierarchical manner from the lower to the higher order. In essence, he believed that once a given level of need is satisfied, it no longer serves to motivate man.

Moslow identified five levels in his need hierarchy as shown in figure.

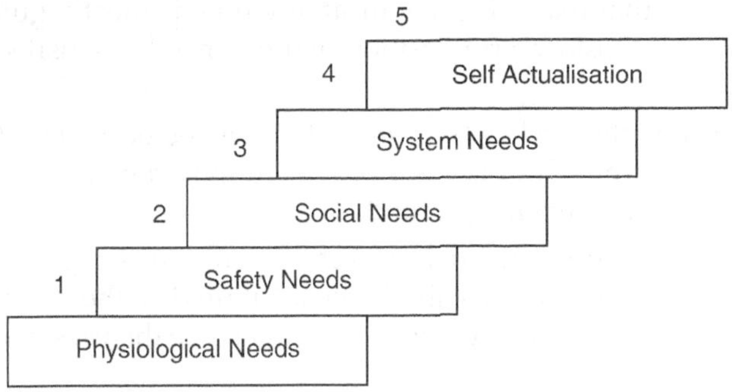

Maslow's Need Hierarchy

1. ***Physiological Needs.*** These needs are basic to human life and, hence, include food, clothing, shelter, air, water and other necessities of life. These needs are relate to the survival and maintenance of human life. They exert tremendous influence on human behaviour. These needs are to be met first at least partly before higher level needs emerge. Once physiological needs are satisfied, they no longer motivate the man.
2. ***Safety Needs.*** After satisfying the physiological needs, the next needs felt are called safety and security needs. These needs find expression such desires as economic security and protection from physical dangers. Meeting these needs requires more money and hence, the individual is prompted to work more. Like physiological needs, these become inactive once they are satisfied.
3. ***Social Needs.*** Man is a social being. He is therefore, interested in socal interaction, companionship, belongingness, etc. It is this socializing and belongingness why individuals prefer to work in groups and especially older people go to work.
4. ***Esteem Needs.*** These need refer to self-esteem and resolve respect. They include such needs, which indicate self-confidence, achievement, competence, knowledge and independence. The fulfillment of esteem needs leads to self-confidence, strength and capability of being useful in the organization. However, inability to fulfil these needs results in feelings like inferiority, weakness and helplessness.
5. ***Self-Actualization Needs.*** This level represents the culmination of all the lower, intermediate and higher needs of human beings. In other words, the final step under the need hierarchy model is the need for self-actualization. This refers to fulfillment.

According to Maslow, the human needs follow a definite sequence of domination. The second need does not arise until the first is reasonably satisfied, the third need does not emerge until the first two needs have been reasonably satisfied and so on.

Criticism made against this theory is as follows:

1. The needs may or may not follow a definite hierarchical order. So to say, there may overlapping in need hierarchy. For example, even if safety need is not satisfied, the social need may emerge.
2. The need priority model may not apply at all times in all places.

3. Researches show that man's behaviour at any time is mostly guided by multiplicity of behaviour. Hence, Moslow's preposition that one need is satisfied at one time is also of doubtful validity.
4. In case of some people, the level of motivation may be permanently lower. For example, a person suffering from chronic unemployment may remain satisfied for the rest of his life if only he/she can get enough food.

Notwithstanding, Maslow's need hierarchy theory has received wide recognition, particularly among practicing managers. This can be attributed to the theory's intuitive logic and easy to understand. One researcher came to the conclusion those theories that are intuitively strong die-hard.

4.2.6.2. Herzberg's Motivation Hygiene Theory

The psychologist Frederik Herzberg extended the work of Maslow and proposed a new motivation theory popularly known as Herzberg's Motivation Hygiene (Two-Factor) Theory. Herzberg conducted a widely reported motivation study of 200 accountants and engineers employed by firms in an around Western Pennsylvania. He asked these people to describe two important incidents at their jobs:

(*a*) When did you feel particularly good about your job? and

(*b*) When did you feel exceptionally bad about your job?

He asked the critical incident method of obtaining data. The responses when analyzed were found quite interesting and fairly consistent. The replies respondents gave when they felt good about their jobs were significantly different from the replies given when they felt bad. Reported good feelings were generally associated with job satisfaction whereas bad feelings with job dissatisfaction. Herzberg labeled the job satisfies motivators and he called job dissatisfies hygiene or maintenance factors. Taken together, the motivators and hygiene factors have become known as Herzberg's two-factor theory of motivation.

Herzberg's motivational and hygiene factors have shown in this table.

Hygiene: Job dissatisfaction	Motivators: Job satisfaction
	Achievement Recognition Work itself Responsibility Advancement Growth
Company Policy and Administration Supervision Interpersonal Relations Working Conditions Salary Status Security	

According to Herzberg, the opposite of satisfaction is not dissatisfaction. The underlying reason, he says, is that removal of dissatisfying characteristics from a job does not necessarily make the job satisfying. He believes in the existence of a dual continuum. The opposite of 'satisfaction' is no satisfaction and the opposite of 'dissatisfaction' is no 'dissatisfaction'.

According to Herzberg, today's motivators are tomorrow's hygiene because the latter stop influencing the behaviour of persons when they get them. Accordingly one's hygiene may be the motivator of another.

Criticism of Herzberg's model

1. People generally tend to take credit themselves when things go well. They blame failure on the external environment.
2. The theory basically explains job satisfaction not motivation.
3. Even job satisfaction is not measured on an overall basis. It is not unlikely that a person may dislike part of his/her job, still thinks the job acceptable.
4. This theory neglects situational variable to motivate an individual.

Regardless of criticisms, Herzberg "two factor motivation theory' has been widely read and a few managers seem unfamiliar with his recommendations. The main use of his recommendations lies in planning and controlling of employee's work.

Distinction between Maslow's and Herzberg's Theories

Both Maslow and Herzberg theories focus on motivational factors. However, both differ from each other in their approaches. As discussed earlier, Maslow's motivation theory is based on the hierarchy of needs. According to this theory, only unsatisfied needs motivate individuals. Once a need is satisfied, it ceases to be a motivating factor. But Herberg's motivation theory is based on motivational and hygiene of maintenance factors. According to Herzberg, hygiene or maintenance factors prevent job dissatisfaction but do not provide motivation to workers. In his view, Maslow's lower order needs like physiological, safety and social needs act as hygiene or maintenance factors.

4.2.6.3. McClelland's Need Theory

Another well-known need-based theory of motivation, as opposed to hierarchy of needs or satisfaction-dissatisfaction, is the theory developed by McClelland and his associates. McClelland developed his theory based on Henry Murray's long list of motives and manifest needs used in early studies of personality. His theory focuses on Murray's three needs: Achievement, Power and Affiliation. They are defined as follows:

- *Need for Achievement:* This is the drive to excel, to achieve in relation to a set of standard, and to strive to succeed. In other words, need for achievement is a behaviour directed toward competition with a standard of excellence. McClelland found that people with a high need for achievement perform better than those with a moderate or low need for achievement and noted regional/national differences in achievement motivation. Through his research, McClelland identified the following three characteristics of high need achievers.

  1. High need achievers have a strong desire to assume personal responsibility for performing a task or finding a solution to a problem.

2. High need achievers tend to set moderately difficult goals and take calculated risks.
3. High need achievers have a strong desire for performance feedback.

- ***Need for Power:*** The need for power is concerned with making an impact on others, the desire to influence others, the urge to change people, land the desire to make a difference in life. People with high need for power are people who like to be in control of people and events. This results in ultimate satisfaction to man.

  People who have a high need for power are characterized by:

  1. A desire to influence and direct somebody else.
  2. A desire to exercise control over others.
  3. A concern for maintaining leader-follower relations.

- ***Need for Affiliation:*** The need for affiliation is defined as a desire to establish and maintain friendly and warm relations with other people. The need for affiliation, in many ways, is similar to Maslow's social needs. The people with high need for affiliation have these characteristics.

  1. They have a strong desire for acceptance and approval from others.
  2. They tend to conform to the wishes of those people whose friendship and companionship they value.
  3. They value feeling of others.

4.2.6.4. Vroom's Expectancy Theory

Victor Vroom in his Expectancy Theory offers one of the most widely accepted explanations of motivation. It is a cognitive process theory of motivation. The theory is founded on the basic notions that people will be motivated to exert a high level of effort when they believe there are relationships between the effort they put forth, the performance they achieve, and the outcomes/rewards they receive.

The relationships between notions of effort, performance, and reward are depicted in Figure. Thus, the key constructs in the Vroom's expectancy theory of motivation are:

1. ***Valence.*** Valence, according to Vroom, means the value or strength one places on a particular outcome or reward.
2. ***Expectancy.*** It relates efforts to performance.
3. ***Instrumentality.*** By instrumentality, Vroom means, the belief that performance is related to rewards.

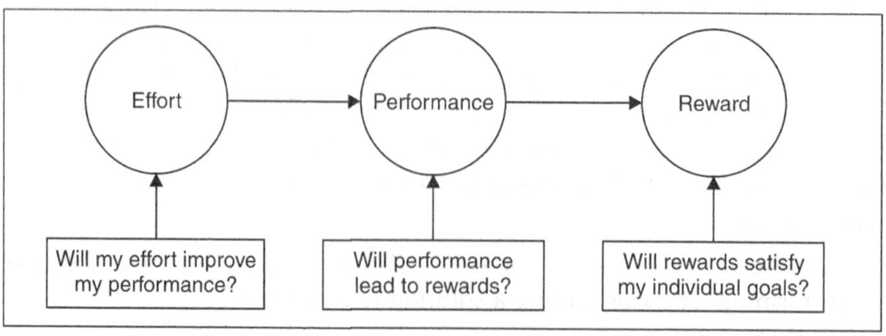

Thus, Vroom's motivation can also be expressed in the form of an equation as follows.

Motivation = Valence × Expectancy × Instrumentality

Being the model multiplicative in nature, all the three variables must have high positive values to imply motivated performance choices. If any one of the variables approaches to zero level, the possibility of the so motivated performance also touches zero level.

However, Vroom's expectancy theory has its critics. The important ones are:

1. Critics like Porter and Lawler lebeled it as a theory of cognitive hedonism which proposes that individual cognitively chooses the course of action that leads to the greatest degree of pleasure or the smallest degree of pain.
2. The assumption that people are rational and calculating makes the theory idealistic.
3. The expectancy theory does not describe individual and situational differences.

But the valence, or value people place on various rewards varies. For example, one employee prefers salary to benefits, whereas another person prefers to just the reverse. The valence for the same reward varies from situation to situation.

In spite of all these critics, the greatest point in the expectancy theory is that it explains why a significant segment of workforce exerts low levels of efforts in carrying out job responsibilities.

4.2.6.5. Porter and Lawler's Expectancy Theory

In fact, Porter and Lawler's theory is an improvement over Vroom's expectancy theory. They posit that motivation does not equal satisfaction or performance. The model suggested by them encounters some of the simplistic traditional assumptions made about the positive relationship between satisfaction and performance. They proposed a multi-variety model to explain the complex relationship that exists between satisfaction and performance. What is the main point in Porter and Lawler's model is that effort or motivation does not lead directly to performance.

It is, in fact, mediated by abilities and traits and by role perceptions. Ultimately, performance leads to satisfaction. This is depicted in the following figure.Let us briefly discuss the main elements of the model:

- *Effort:* Effort refers to the amount of energy an employee exerts on a given task. How much effort an employee will put in a task is determined by two factors:

  (*i*) value of reward and (*ii*) perception of effort-reward probability.

- *Performance:* One's effort leads to his/her performance. Both may be equal or may not be. However, the amount of performance is determined by the amount of labour and the ability and role perception of the employee. Thus, if an employee possesses less ability and/or makes wrong role perception, his/her performance may be low in spite of his putting in great efforts.
- *Satisfaction:* Performance leads to satisfaction. The level of satisfaction depends upon the amount of rewards one achieves. If the amount of actual rewards meet or exceed perceived equitable rewards, the employee will feel satisfied. On the contrary, if actual rewards fall short of perceived ones, he/she will be dissatisfied.

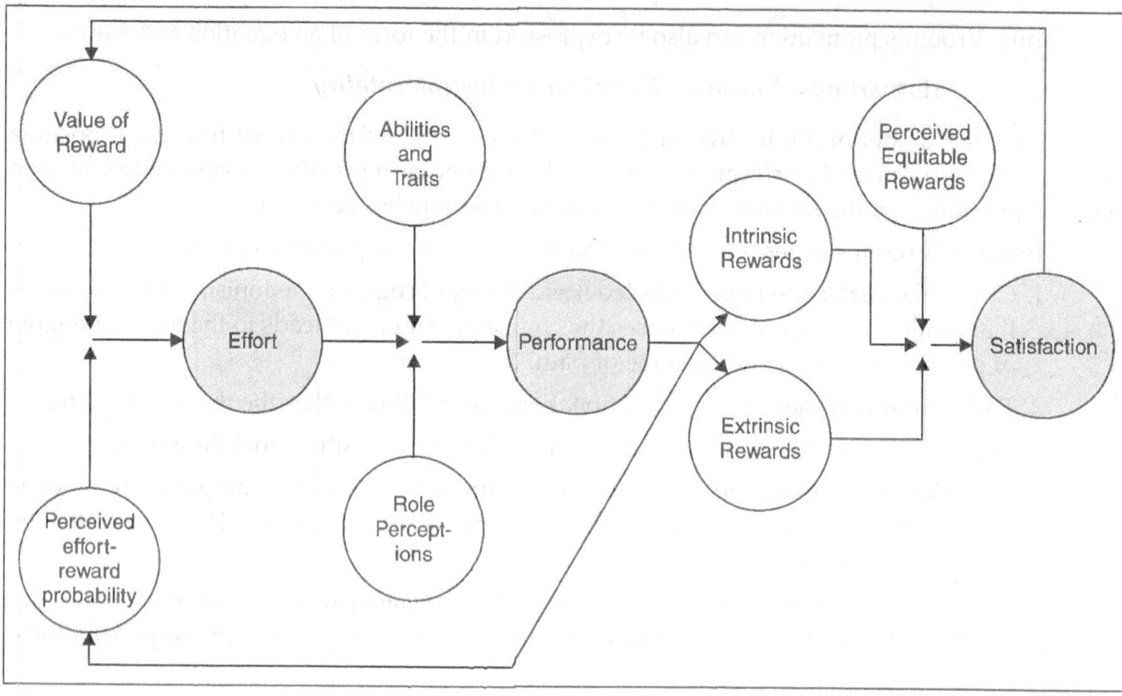

Rewards may be of two kinds–intrinsic and extrinsic rewards. Examples of intrinsic rewards are such as a sense of accomplishment and self-acualisation. As regards extrinsic rewards, these may include working conditions and status. A fair degree of research supports that the intrinsic rewards are much more likely to produce attitudes about satisfaction that are related to performance.

There is no denying of the fact that the motivation model proposed by Porter and Lawler is quite complex than other models of motivation. In fact, motivation itself is not a simple cause effect relationship rather it is a complex phenomenon. Porter and Lawler have attempted to measure variables such as the values of possible rewards, the perception of effort-rewards probabilities, and role perceptions in deriving satisfaction. They recommended that the managers should carefully reassess their reward system and structure. The effort-performance-reward satisfaction should be made integral to the entire system of managing men in organizations.

4.2.6.6. McGregor's Theory (X & Y Theory)

Prof. Douglas McGregor has introduced two theories in his famous book, "The Human side of Enterprise". They are called 'X' theory and 'Y' theory.

X-Theory

This theory is based on "papa knows best". In other words, a manager has thorough knowledge and excludes workers from decision-making process. A manager has authority or power to take decisions. The workers should follow whatever decisions are taken by the managers.

Assumptions of X-Theory

- Workers have an aversion to work inherently.
- Workers may find a way to postpone the work completion in laziness.

- Workers may do the job half-heartedly.
- Fear of punishment can motivate the workers into action.
- The worker may know the hazards of non-performance of a work.
- No worker is ready to accept any responsibility.
- There is a need for explaining the consequences of being inactive.
- Workers are not interested in achievement. They prefer to maintain status quo.
- A worker prefers to be directed by others.
- Workers hate to improve their efficiency. The reason is that they fear losing their present job.
- Workers is also one of the factors of production and does not deserve any special treatment.
- Worker lacks integrity.
- Workers avoids taking decision whenever necessary.

X-Theory is regarded as the means to supervise and control the workers. Decision-making in all the fields is entrusted with the managers. Workers are allowed to express their suggestions and emotions. But the decisions are taken by managers and workers are forced to follow the decisions.

Y-Theory

Y-Theory is just opposite to X-Theory. So, X-theory is considered as traditional theory and Y-theory as modern theory. Y-Theory emphasizes the importance of workers in the accomplishment of enterprise objectives.

Assumptions of Y-Theory

- The average human being has the tendency to work. A job is as natural just like a play.
- Once the worker understands the purpose of job, he may extend his cooperation for job completion.
- Worker can put in his best efforts for the accomplishment of enterprise objectives early.
- Worker has self-direction, self-motivation, self-discipline and self-control.
- If the management prepares right motivation scheme, the worker is ready to accept extra responsibility.
- The existing worker has competence to work and can take right decisions.
- A worker expects recognition of the successful accomplishment of task.
- A worker may exhibit his efficiency even for non-monetary rewards such as participation in decision-making, increased responsibility etc.
- The potentialities of human beings are not fully utilized by any industry.

According to Y-Theory, a worker has integrity and readiness to work hard. He is willing to participate in the decision-making process and shows a sense of creativity and imagination. So, X-Theory may say to be a negative and pessimistic one and Y-Theory may say to be positive and optimistic.

4.3. COMMUNICATION

The word 'communication' is derived from the Latin word 'Communis' which means common. If a person affects a communication, he has established a common ground of understanding.

> *"Communication in its simplest form is conveying of information from one person to another."*
>
> *—Hudson*

Stephen P Robbins views that communication refers to transference and understanding of meaning. Thus, communication means transference of messages or exchange of ideas, facts, opinion or feelings by two or more persons. It is the act of making one's ideas and opinions known to others. Thus, communication does not simply involve sending of a message to one person. It also involves the receiver listening to it, and responding to it or acting according to it.

4.3.1. Nature of Communication

1. Communication involves two parties, one who transmits and one who receives the message.
2. The two respective parties must have ability to convey and listen to what the sender to communicate.
3. Communication includes sending the message and also receiving the response to the message.
4. The message may be conveyed verbally, in writing, by means of signs, gestures of symbols.
5. Communication is a continuous process. It pervades the entire organization.

4.3.2. Purpose of Communication

The purpose of communication in an enterprise is to effect change–to influence action toward the welfare of the enterprise. Communication is needed to

- Establish and disseminate goals of an enterprise
- Develop plans for their achievement
- Organize human and other resources
- Select, develop and appraise members of the organization
- Lead, direct, motivate and create a climate in which people want to contribute and
- Control performance.

4.3.3. Process of Communication

The process of communication includes the following seven elements:

1. Communicator
2. Encoding
3. Message
4. Medium
5. Decoding
6. Receiver, and
7. Feedback.

These are shown in the following figure.

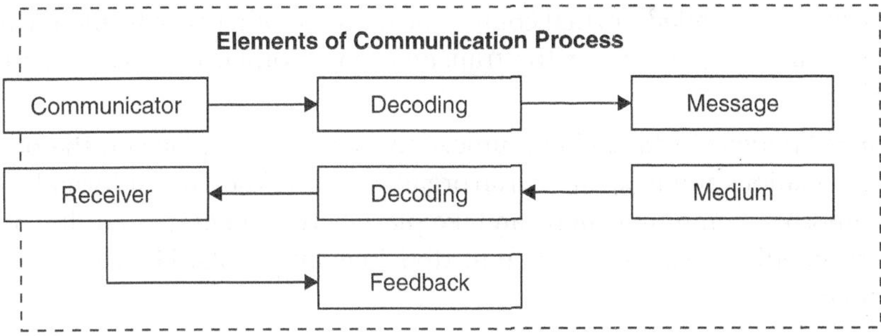

1. ***Communicator.*** The communication process begins with who has an intended message to communicate. The characteristics of the communicator influence the communication process.
2. ***Encoding.*** It refers to converting a communication message into symbolic form. Encoding is necessary because information can only be transmitted from communicator to receiver through the symbols or gestures.
3. ***Message.*** The message is the actual physical product from the source of encoding. When we speak, the speech is the message we write. When we gesture, the movements of our arms, the expressions on our face are the message.
4. ***Medium.*** Medium is a channel through which a communication message travels. Medium is the link that connects the communicator (sender) and the receiver. face-to-face verbal communication, use of telephone, use of memorandum, notice, circulars, statements, etc. are the various means available as media of communication. Besides, non-verbal media like signals, symbols, gestures, etc. may also be used.
5. ***Decoding.*** Translating the sender's message by the receiver is called decoding. Decoding is the process by which the receiver draws meaning from the symbols encoded by the communicator or sender.
6. ***Receiver.*** The person who receives the message is called receiver. The communicator process is incomplete without the existence of receiver of message.
7. ***Feedback.*** The actual response of the receiver to the message communicated to him is known as "feedback". In other words, if a communicator or sender decodes the message that he encodes, if the message is put back into his system, we have feedback.

4.3.4. Channels of Communication

The channel is the medium or path through which the message travels. The channels of communication can be divided in the following three bases:

- Based on Relationship
- Based on Direction of Flow, and
- Based on Method used.

(I) Based on Relationship

(*a*) ***Formal Communication.*** The channels of communications established formally by the management are called 'formal communication'. In other words, the formal channels of communication are used for the transmission of official messages within or outside organization.

(*b*) ***Informal Communication.*** Communication, which takes place on the basis of informal or social relations among people in an organization, is known as informal communication. Thus, informal communication can take place between persons cutting across positions held by people working in different divisions and units. Hence, it is also known as 'Grapevine'.

(II) Based on Direction of Flow

1. ***Horizontal Communication.*** It refers to transmission of information among positions of the same level. This facilitates coordination among peers or people working on same levels.
2. ***Upward Communication.*** When communication flows from lower-level employees to higher-level employees, it called upward communication. Upward level communication encourages employees to participate in the decision-making process and submit valuable ideas and suggestions.
3. ***Downward Communication.*** It refers to the flow of information from higher level to lower level employees. Such communication may consist of verbal messages, conveying orders, policies, procedures, or written matters conveyed through notices, circulars etc.
4. ***Diagonal Communication.*** Diagonal communication refers to flow of messages between persons who are in positions at different levels of hierarchy and also in different departments. This type of communication takes place under special circumstances.

(III) Based on Method used

1. ***Verbal Communication.*** When the message is conveyed orally, it is called verbal communication. It produces in communication a personal touch. Verbal communication is the most economical both in terms of time and money. However, its greatest drawback, if any, is its non-applicability especially when the communicator and receiver are at places far away from one another and the number of persons to be communicated is large.
2. ***Written Communication.*** Communication that takes place between people in written form is called written form. Formal communication is usually in written form such as orders, instructions, reports, bulletins, etc. Communication being in written form is permanent, tangible and verifiable. Limitations of written communication are that it is time consuming, lacks personal touch and unfolds the secrecy about the written message.
3. ***Gestural Communication.*** When the message is transmitted through some gestures, it is called gestural communication. People use different gestures such as moving hands and eyes to communicate their views, ideas, etc. If the superior pats his subordinate on his back, it is understood as appreciation for work.

4.3.5. Communication Networks

In organizations, communication flows among groups of individuals in different patterns. The five most common communication networks are: Circle, wheel, Chain, Y Network and All channel networks.

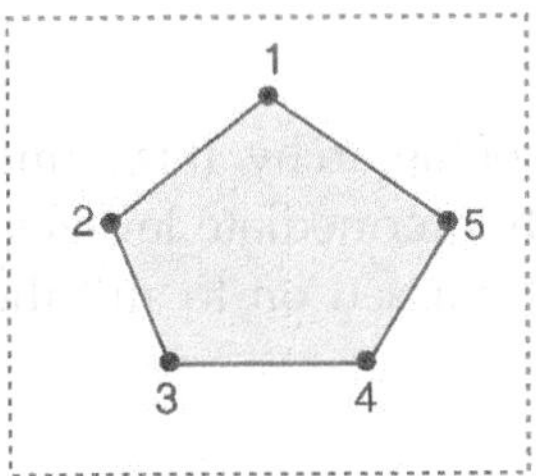

Circle

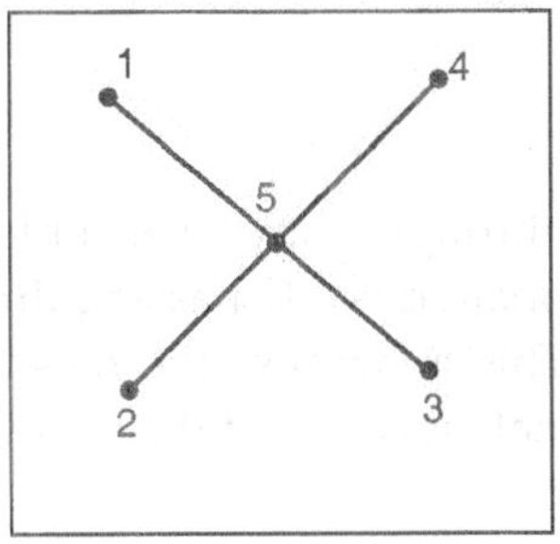

Wheel

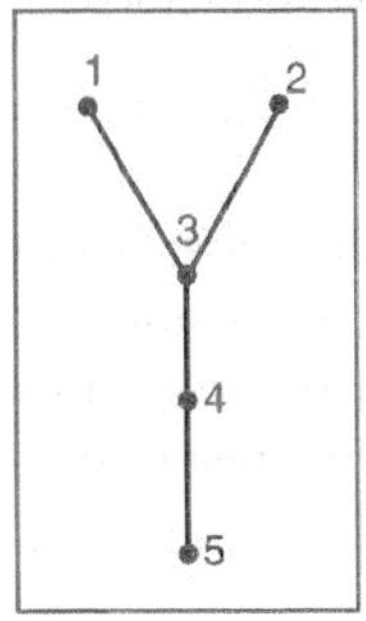

Y

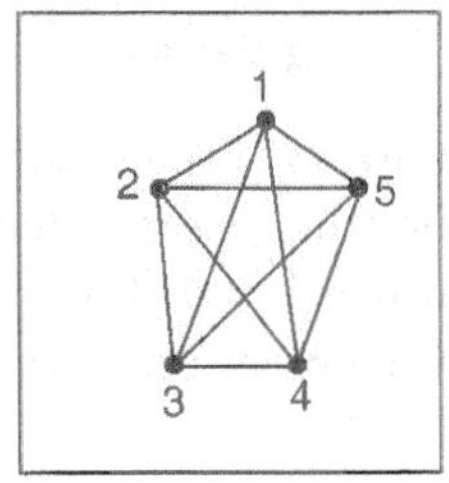

All channel

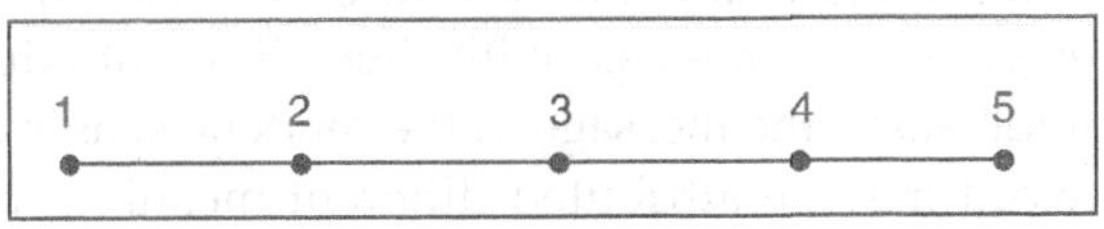

Chain

Circle. It is the network where each members of the group can interact with the adjoining member. The circle network is highly decentralized because each position can communicate directly with two other positions in the network. No one can communicate directly with everyone.

Wheel. In case of wheel network, one person (a supervisor for example) can communicate with (say) four workers, but the workers do not communicate with each other. The wheel relies on the leader to act as the central control for all the group's communication. Since, all communication passes through the center position, the wheel is the most centralized communication network.

Chain. In this network, one person transmits information to another as per the chain in the organizational hierarchy. For example, the president informs the vice-president who then passes on the same information to the head of the department, who tells his/her manager, who passes on to the supervisor, who then informs the employee.

Y Network. In this type of network, two people report to a superior or boss who occupies two positions as shown in the figure.

All-Channel. The all-channel network permits all group members to actively communicate with each other.

4.3.6. Barriers to Communication

Barriers to communication are factors that come in the way of effective communication, Some Barriers to communication are filtering of the message, language, physical separation, status differences and emotions.

Lack of Planning

Good communication seldom happens by change. Too often people start talking and writing without first thinking, planning and stating the purpose of the message. Giving the reasons for a directive, selecting the most appropriate channel and choosing proper timing can greatly improve understanding and reduce resistance to change.

Filtering Barrier

In formal organizations, the message travels through many layers or levels of hierarchy. It is found that the message tends to be distorted or impaired while passing through intermediate levels in upward and downward communications. This is because the message is passed on to suit the convenience or serve the interest of the ultimate receiver of the message.

Language Barrier

Language is a central element in communication. It may pose a barrier if its use obscures meaning and distorts intent. The receivers of the message with their different educational and cultural backgrounds find it hard to understand the message in the senders' senses due to jargons used in the message language. The word may be attributed different meanings by the sender and the receiver of the message. This is known as the problem of semantics.

Physical Separation Barrier

The physical separation of people in the work environment poses a barrier to communication. Physical distance between the sender and the receiver of any message serves an obstacle to effective communication. This is because the difficulty involved in evaluating whether the receiver has understood, accepted, and acted upon the message sent to him when his workplace is far away from that of the sender of the message.

Status Barrier

Status differences related to power and the organizational hierarchy pose another barrier to communication among people at work, especially within manager-employee pairs. It is due to the status difference that subordinates often suppress or withhold information which may not be liked by their superiors, or pass on distorted information to please their superiors. On the other side, status consciousness of the superiors prevents them from fully communicating information to their subordinates.

Emotional Barrier

When people are eloquent with emotions, it influences their understanding of the message accordingly. Psychological barriers do also impair effectiveness of communication. When the subordinates hold favourable image of the superior, they become psychologically more inclined to accept and respond positively to the message sent by the superior. Obviously, it does not happen so when they have an unfavourable image of their superior. The image is built on the basis of experience and interaction between the superior and the subordinate. Any change when its effects are uncertain also creates psychological barriers to effective communication in an organization.

4.3.7. Suggestions for Making Communication Effective

- *Language:* While preparing the communication message, its language should be relatively simple and the ability of the receiver to interpret the message accurately should be kept in view. Efforts should be made to explain abstract ideas and avoid vague expressions.
- *Regulating Flow of Communication:* Priority of messages to be communicated should be determined so that the managers may concentrate on more important messages of high priority. Similarly, the messages received should be edited and condensed, to the extent possible, to reduce the chances of overlooking or ignoring important messages.
- *Feedback:* Communication is complete when it receives feedback. Feedback may include the receiver's response in terms of acceptance and understanding of the message, his/her action, and the result achieved. Thus, the two-way communication is considered to be more helpful in establishing mutual understanding then one-way communication.
- *Repetition:* Repetition of message helps to improve effectiveness of communication. It helps the listener interpret messages that are ambiguous, unclear, or too difficult to understand the first time they heard. Repetition also helps to avoid the problem of forgetting.
- *Restraint over Emotions:* A strong feeling and emotions on the part of either the sender or receiver of the message distort the meaning of the message, one may therefore, defers the communication for some time.
- *Mutual Trust and Faith:* Communication become effective having mutual trust and faith between the sender and receiver of the message. The honesty of the purpose is the best means breeding trust and faith between two parties i.e. sender and receiver.
- *Listening Carefully:* A receiver-listener needs to be patient mentally well composed, and avoids distractions while receiving the message. He/she should seek clarification, if necessary on the message. At the same time, the sender of the message must also be prepared to listen to what the receiver has to say, and respond to his questions, if any.

4.3.8. Electronic Media in Communication

Electronic equipment includes mainframe computers, minicomputers, personal computers, electronic mail system, and electronic typewriters as well as cellular telephones for making telephone calls from cars and beeper for keeping in contact with the office.

Telecommunication

Although telecommunication is just emerging a number of companies have already effectively utilized the new technology in a variety of ways as shown by the following examples.

- *A large bank supplies hardware and software to its customers so that they can easily transfer funds to their suppliers.*

- *Several banks now make bank by phone services available even to individuals.*
- *Facsimile main service ensures delivery of a document across the country within hours.*
- *The computerized airline reservation system facilitates making travel arrangements.*
- *Many firms have detailed personnel information—including performance appraisals and career development plans-in a data bank.*

Teleconferencing

Teleconferencing involves a wide variety of systems, including audio systems, audio systems with snapshots displayed on the video monitor, and live video systems. When a group of people interacts with each other by means of audio and video media with moving or still pictures, the group is said to be in 'teleconference'.

Full motion video is frequently used to hold meetings among managers. Not only do they hear each other, but they can also see each other's expressions or discuss some visual display.

Advantages

Some of the potential advantage of teleconferencing includes savings in travel expenses and travel time. There is no need to make travel plans long in advance. Because meetings can be held more frequently, communication is improved between, for example headquarters and geographically scattered divisions.

Disadvantages

Because of the case in arranging meetings in this manner, they may be held more often than necessary. Teleconferencing is still considered as a poor substitute for meeting with other persons face-to-face. Despite these limitations, an increased use of teleconferencing is likely in the future.

Chapter 5 CONTROLLING

5.1. INTRODUCTION

The managerial function of controlling is the measurement and correction of performance in order to make sure that enterprise objectives and the plans desired to attain them are accomplished. Planning and controlling are closely related. In fact, some writers on management think that these functions cannot be separated. Planning and controlling may be viewed as the blades of a pair of scissors; the scissors cannot work unless there are two blades. Without objectives and planes, control is not possible, because performance has to be compared against some established criteria.

Controlling is the function of every manager from the president to supervisor. Some managers particularly at lower levels forget that the primary responsibility for the exercise of control rests in every manager charged with the execution of plans. Occasionally, because of the authority of upper level managers and their resultant responsibility, top and upper level control is so emphasized that people assume that little controlling is needed at lower levels. Although the scope of control varies among managers, those at all levels have responsibility for the execution of plans and control is therefore an essential managerial function at every level.

5.2. DEFINITION

"Control is checking current performance against predetermined standards contained in the plans with a view to ensuring adequate progress and satisfactory performance."

—E. F L Breach.

"Controlling is the measurement and correction of performance in order to make sure that enterprise objectives and the plans devised to attain them are accomplished."

—Harold Koontz

5.3. NATURE/CHARACTERISTICS OF CONTROL

1. *Control process is universal.* Control is essential function in any organization whether it is an industrial unit, university, government office, hospital etc.
2. *Control is a continuous process.* Control is a never-ending activity on the part of managers. It is a non-stop process. The manager watches the operation of the management and to see whether they are going towards the desired end and if not actions are not taken to correct them.
3. *Control is action based.* Action is essential element of the control. It is the action, which ensures performance according to the decided standards.
4. *Control is forward looking.* Control is linked with future not past. A proper control system prevents losses, minimizes wastages. It acts as a preventive measure.
5. *Control is closely linked with planning.* Plan gives the direction to various business activities while control verifies and measures the performance of these activities and suggests proper measures to remove the deviations.

5.4. NEED FOR CONTROL

A control system is needed for three purposes:

- To measure progress
- To uncover deviation and
- To indicate corrective action.

To Measure Progress

There is a close link between planning and controlling the organizations operations. The planning process, the fundamental goals and objection of the organization and the methods for attaining them should be established. The control process measures progress towards there goals. As Henry Fayol clearly recognized decades ago. "In an undertaking, control consists in verifying whether everything occurs in conformity with the plan adopted, the construction issued and principles established." As the navigator continually takes readings to ascertain where he is relative to a planned course, so does the manager take readings to see where his enterprise or department is on the charted and predetermined?

To Discover Deviations

Once a business organisation is set into motion towards its specific objectives, events occur that tend to pull it "off target". A successful control process is one that effect connections to the organization before the deviations become serious. Major events, which tend to pull an organization 'off target' are as follows.

Change: Change is an integral part of almost organisations environment. Markets shift, new products emerge new materials are discovered and new regulation are passed. The control function enables managers to detect changes that are affecting their organizations product as services. They can then move to cope with the threats or opportunities that these changes represent.

Complaints: Today's vast and complex organisations, with geographically separated plants and decentralized operations make control a necessity. Diversified product lines need to be watched closely to ensure that quality and profitability are being maintained. Sales in different retail outlets need to be recorded accurately and analyzed, the organisations various markets. Foreign and domestic require close monitoring.

Mistakes: Managers and their subordinates very often commit mistakes. For example, wrong parts are ordered, wrong pricing decisions are made, problems are diagnosed incorrectly and so on. A control system enables manager to catch the mistakes before they become serious.

Delegation: When manager delegate authority to subordinates, their responsibilities to their own superiors is not reduced. They only was manager can determine if their subordinates are accomplishing the tasks that have been delegated to them is by implementing a system of control. Without such a system, manager will not be able to check on their subordinate's progress, and so not be able to take corrective action until often a failure has occurred.

To Indicate Corrective Action

Controls are needed to indicate corrective actions. They may reveal, for example, that plans need to be redrawn or goals need to be modified or there is need for reassignment or clarification of duties for additional staffing. When the corrective action indicated by the control system is implemented, the loop in the system classes as in the operating principle of a thermostat as shown below:

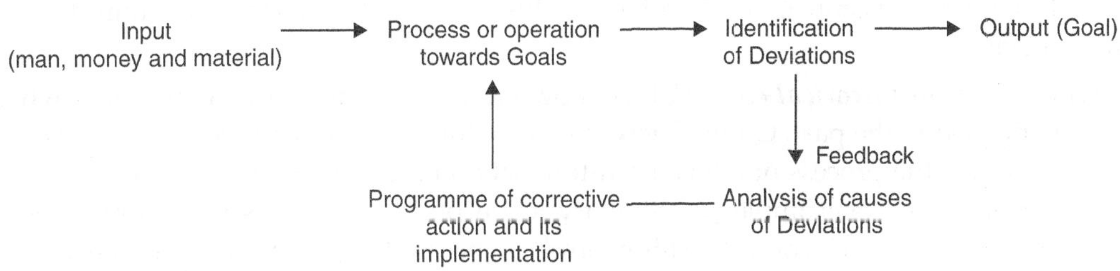

5.5. SIGNIFICANCE AND LIMITATIONS OF CONTROL

5.5.1. Significance of Control

(*i*) ***Policy verification.*** Control helps to review, revise and update the plans. In this process organization and management can verify the quality of various policies.

(*ii*) ***Adjustments in operations.*** A control system acts as an adjustment in organizational operations. Control provides this clue by finding out whether plans are being observed and suitable progress towards the objective is being made to correct any deviations if necessary.

(*iii*) ***Psychological pressure.*** Control process puts a psychological pressure on the individual for better performance. The sound control system inspires employees to work hard and give better performance.

(*iv*) ***Coordination.*** Control helps to emerge the coordination of the subordinates in the organization. Control ensures coordination of the activities of different department through unity of direction.

(*v*) ***Employee morale.*** Control creates an atmosphere of order and discipline in the organization. Control contributes order and discipline in the organization.

(*vi*) ***Efficiency and effectiveness.*** Proper control ensures organizational efficiency and effectiveness. The organization is effective if it is able to achieve its objective. Since control focuses on the achievement or organizational objectives. It necessarily leads to organizational effectiveness.

5.5.2. Limitations of Control

- Control is expensive and time-consuming process.
- Control cannot consider the external factors such as technological changes, political factors, social changes, government procedures etc.
- Human behaviour and employee morale also can not be measured.

5.6. TYPES OF CONTROL

There are three types of control viz. feed back or historical control, concurrent control and feed forward control.

(*a*) ***Feedback or historical control.*** It is known as post action control. It examines what has happened in the past. On the basis of this feedback corrective action is taken. Feedback control is the process of adjusting future action on the basis of information about past performance. For examples, disciplinary action, budgetary results and quality inspections are some feed back controls. This control can be used to plan future with the aid of past errors or success.

(*b*) ***Concurrent control.*** It is as real time control. It provides measures for taking corrective action or doing adjustments while the programme meets any obstacle. Organization control chart is an example of concurrent control. For example riding a bicycle you must adjust yourself depending on the turns in the road and keep your vehicle up right and move towards your aim.

(*c*) ***Feed forward control.*** This control involves evaluation of inputs and taking corrective actions before a particular operation is completed. It is preventive in nature. This control allows corrective action to be taken in advance of the problem. For example cash budget in the organization is this type of control. The finance manager prepares the next five-year flow of cash budget in the organization. If there is a shortage of finance for particular month he is responsible to arrange for bank loan or other alternatives.

5.7. ESSENTIALS OF EFFECTIVE CONTROL SYSTEM

The essentials of an effective control system or the control process are as follows:

Suitable

The control system should be appropriate to the nature and needs of the activity. Controls used in the sales department will be different from those used in finance and personnel. Similarly, a machine-based method of production requires a control system, which is different from the system that is used in labour intensive methods of production. Hence, every concern should evolve such a control system as would serve its specific needs.

Timely and forward looking

The control system should be such as to enable the subordinates to inform their superior. Expeditiously about the threatened deviation and failures. The feedback system should be as short and quick as possible. This would help the manager to take immediate corrective action before the problem occurs. A manager would surely prefer a forecast of what will probably happen next week as next month–even though this contains a margin of error–to a report, accurate to several decimal points, of the past about which he can do nothing.

That this is possible is illustrated by such forward-looking devices as cash control. Cash control forecasts tells about cash needs well in advance and the manager is enabled to take corrective action immediately.

Objective and comprehensible

The control system should be both; objective and understandable, objective controls specify the expected results in clear and definite terms and leave little room for arguments by the employee. They avoid red tape and provide employees with direct access to any additional information, which they may need to perform their task. Employees are not made to go up and down the hierarchy to get the information.

Flexible

The control system should flexible so that it can be adjusted to suit the needs of any change in the environment.

Economical

Economy is another requirement of every control system. The benefit derived from a control system should be more than the cost involved in implementing it. To spend a dollar to protect 99% is not control. It is waste. Eighty years ago this was clearly understood by the men who built Sears, Roebuck, the worlds biggest retail shop.

In the early days of the mail-order business the money in incoming orders was not counted. The orders were weighted, unopened. (These were, of course, Roebuck had run enough tests to know what average weights correspond to overall amounts of money and this was sufficient control.

Prescriptive and operation

A control system in order to be effective and adequate must not only detect deviations from the standards but should also provide for solutions to the problems that cause deviations. In other words, the system should be prescriptive and operational. It must disclose where failures are occurring. Who is responsible for them and what should be done about them. It must focus more on action than information.

Acceptable to organization member

The system should be acceptable to organisation member. When standards are set unilaterally by upper level manager there is a danger that employees will regard those standards as unreasonably or unrealistic. They may then refuse to meet them. Status differences between individuals also have to be recognized. Individuals who have to report deviations to someone they perceive as a lower level staff member may stop taking the control system seriously.

Reveal exceptions at strategic point

A Control system should be such as to reveal exceptions at strategic points. Small exceptions in certain areas have greater significance than larger deviations in other areas. Five percent deviations from the standard in office labour cost are more important than 20 percent deviations from the standards in the cost of postage stamps. That we can quantify something is no reason for measuring it. The question is "Is this what a managers attention should be focused on?"

Motivate people to high performance

A control system is most effective when it motivates people to high performance. Since most people respond to a challenge, successful meeting a tough standard may well provide a greater sense of accomplishment than meeting an easy standard. However, if a target is so tough that it seems impossible to meet, it will be more likely to discourage than to motivate effort. Standards that are too difficult may, therefore, cause the performance of organization members to decline.

Should not lead to less attention to other aspects

Control over one phase of operations should not lead to less attention to other aspects. For example, if control put pressure on employees to increase output, the quality of work, care of equipment and prevention of waste should not be neglected.

5.8. CONTROL PROCESS

The controlling process involves three steps:

1. Establishing standards.
2. Measuring performance against these standards and
3. Correcting variations from standards and plans.

1. *Establishing Standards.* Plans are the yardsticks against which managers desire controls, the first step in the control process logically would be to establish plans. The step in the control process is to establish standards against which results can be measured. Since entire operations cannot be observed, each organization must first develop its own list of key results areas for the purpose of control. Some key areas in all business organization are

1. Profitability
2. Market Position
3. Productivity
4. Personnel Development
5. Employee Attitude and
6. Public Responsibility

The standards the managers desire to obtain in each key area should be defined as far as possible in quantitative terms. Standards expressed in vague or general terms such as "Costs should be reduced" or "Orders should be executed quickly" are not as specific as "Overheads must be reduced by 12 %" or "All orders must be executed within three working days".

Even standards in areas such as public relations while hard to express in quantitative terms, can be defined more accurately by adding more specific details, about the number and type of customer complaints.

Standards need to be flexible in order to adapt changing conditions. For instance, a new salesman who proves to be an above average performer should have his sales standards adjusted accordingly. Similarly, expected delivery times need to be adjusted if the local highway is being repaired.

Every objective, every goal of the many planning programmes, every policy, every procedure and every budget becomes a standard against which actual performance might be measured. In practice, however, standards trend to be of the following types.

1. ***Physical Standards:*** Such as labour hours per unit of output, units of production per machine hour and so on.
2. ***Cost Standards:*** Such as direct and indirect cost per unit produced, material cost per unit, selling cost per unit of sale etc.
3. ***Revenue Standards:*** Such as average sale per customer, sales per capita in a given market area etc.
4. ***Capital Standards***: Such as the rate of return on capital invested, ratio of current assets to current liabilities etc.
5. ***Intangible Standards:*** Such as competence of managers and employees, success of a public relation programme etc.

Generally speaking, the standards should emphasize the achievements of results more than the conformity to rules and methods. If they do not do so, then people will start giving more importance to rules and methods than to the final results. 'Doing the right things' will give place to 'doing thing right'. This would displace organizational goals.

2. *Measurement of Performance.* It is the second step in the control process. While measuring the performance of standard, the following questions should be kept in mind:

(*i*) What and how to measure?

(*ii*) Why to measure? and

(*iii*) How to check the performance?

Measurement of performance is an easy task when the standards and methods of measuring performance are clear. Peter Drucker pointed out that it is very much desirable to have clear and common measurements in all key areas of business. For example, the performance which is quantitative, can easily be measured in terms of production units, sales units, gross profit, whereas the qualitative performance such as morale, human relations, job satisfaction, etc. cannot easily be measured because of lack of standards. Some techniques are used to measure standards, such as personal observation, sampling, surprise visit, managerial accounting tools and so on.

While measuring performance, comparison of the actual and standard performance should be made in order to find out the deviations and the causes of such deviations. This enables better control and ensures better performance.

3. *Correcting the Deviations.* After comparing the actual performance with the prescribed standards and finding the deviations, the next step that should be taken by the manager is to correct these deviations. Corrective action should be taken without wasting of time so that the normal position can be restored quickly. The manager should also determine the correct causes for deviation. The causes for deviation may be of different types, such as inadequate and poor equipment and machinery, inadequate communication system, lack of motivation of subordinates, defective system of training and selection of personnel, defective system of remuneration etc. The remedial action that should be taken depends on the nature of causes for variation.

5.9. CONTROL TECHNIQUES

A variety of tools and techniques has been used over the years to help managers control the activities in their organizations. We may classify these techniques into Old and New.

5.9.1. Old Control Techniques

Old control techniques are those, which have long been used by managers. Important techniques under this category are budgeting, cost accounting, Break-even analysis, financial statements and ratio analysis, auditing, reports, rules and personal observations. All these techniques are described below:

5.9.1.1. Budgeting

A budget is a statement of anticipated results during a designated time period expressed in financial and non-financial terms. There are three essential steps in the control process include establishing standards comparing results with standards and taking corrective action. In terms of these steps, the preparation of budget is, in effect, the step of establishing standards. In terms of the five types of standards such as physical, cost, revenue, capital and intangible, the budgeting process typically involves the use of cost standards.

The budgeting process begins when top management sets the strategies and goals for the organization. Usually, lower level managers will then devise budgets for their sub-units within these guidelines set by the top management. The supervisors of those managers will then review the budgets; the supervisors will eventually integrate lower level budgets into their own budget and sent it up the chain of command for review. This process continues until the organizations overall budget has been approved by the board of directors. A budget department committee may assist line managers in budget preparation and review.

Types of Budgets

On the basis of the purpose for which budgets are prepared, they may be classified as follows:

1. ***Sales Budget:*** It is a comprehensive sale programme and plan for developing sales. It lays down the sales potential in terms of quantity, value, period, product etc. Sales forecasting is the basis for preparing this budget. The factors to be considered for preparing sales budget are population trend, consumer's purchasing power, price trend of the product, nature of competition, past sales, extent of advertising etc.
2. ***Selling and Distribution Cost Budget:*** This budget lays down the cost of selling and distribution of the product during the budget period. It includes advertising cost, research and development cost, transport cost etc. The sales manager, advertising manager and the distribution manager jointly prepare this budget.
3. ***Production Budget:*** This budget is based on the sales budget. It lays down the quantity of units to be produced during the budget period. The main purpose of their budget is to maintain an optimum balance sales, production and inventory position of the firm.
4. ***Production Cost Budget***: This budget is based on the production budget. It lays down the estimated cost of carrying out production plans.

   Further the production cost budget is sub-divided into various sub-budgets like raw materials budget, labour budget, production over head budget etc.
5. ***Capital Expenditure Budget:*** This budget outlines specifically capital expenditures for plant, machinery, equipment, inventories and other items. It also points out the plans concerning investments, expansion, growth, improvements, replacements etc.
6. ***Cash Budget:*** This budget gives the anticipated receipts and disbursements for the budget period and shows the cash position arising from it. It indicates the requirement of cash at various points of time and helps the management in planning and arranging cash to meet the needs of the business concern. Thus, it ensures that the concern never has any shortage of cash required. Cash budget helps the management in controlling and coordinating the activities, which involve receipt and payment of cash.
7. ***Master Budget:*** A Master budget gives a summary of all the functional budgets and shows how they affect the business as a whole. In other words, it is complied from various subsidiary or functional budget. It provides detailed particulars regarding production, sales, cash, fixed assets etc. The need for a master budget containing a summary of all the subsidiary budgets arise because business concerns are too large to permit the detailed planning of all the aspects of the business in one budget.

Advantages of Budgetary Control

1. The different functional budget clearly indicates the limits for expense and also the results to be achieved limits for expense and also the results to be achieved in a given period. This keeps everybody in the enterprise alert and encourages the optimum use of its resource.
2. Budgets make it possible to co-ordinate the work of the entire organisation. In devising budgets, managers take into account information provided by the sub-units of their organisation, which leads to define and integrate the activities of all the members.
3. Since budgets are generally prepared with the consultation of managers at different levels, they provide to the enterprise the fruit of combined wisdom. Lower level managers are motivated in accepting and meeting budgets that they have had a hand in shaping.
4. The budgetary control brings together the activities of various departments in an overall perspective and this promotes cooperation and team spirit among the employees.
5. Through budgetary control, the deviations from predetermined standards are found out and the management is enabled to take suitable corrective action immediately. This minimizes wastage and losses.
6. The budget system helps people learn from past experience. Once the budget period is over, managers can analyze what occurred, isolate errors and their laws, and take steps to avoid those errors in the next budget period.
7. Budgets improve communication. A plan cannot be put into effect unless it is communicated to those who must carry it out. In the process of developing the budget with those responsible for its implementation, managers can communicate their own objectives and plans must effectively.

Limitations of Budgetary Control

1. Since budgets are used to evaluate results, inefficient employees do not whole heartedly co-operate with the system.
2. Budget estimates sometimes proves to be grossly inaccurate. This renders the budgetary control system totally ineffective.
3. Budgets are mostly inflexible and rigid and do not respond to internal or external environmental changes. The standards once fixed are allowed to continue for several years.
4. Budgets are of little help in handling the here-and-now problems that supervisions have. They are useful only in analyzing the past and charting the future.
5. A budgetary control programme may sometimes become very cumbersome and unduly expensive.
6. A good manager is discouraged from taking initiative and undertaking activities for which provision has not been made in the budget, even though they are useful for the enterprise. On the other hand, a bad manager can hide his inefficiency behind the budget. This is because the budgets have a way of growing from proceeded. An amount once spent becomes a floor for future budgets. Manager asks much more than they need.

Zero Base Budgeting

"A planning and budgeting process which require each manager to justify his entire budget request in detail from scratch (hence Zero Base) and shifts the burden of proof to each manager, to justify why he should spend money at all. The approach requires that all activities be analysed in decision 'packages' which are evaluated by systematic analysis and ranked in the order of importance."

—Peter. A. Phyrr.

5.9.1.2. Standard Costing

The cost of production determines the profit earned by an enterprise. In view of this fact, the modern management has given much importance to cost accounting and cost control. Standard costing is one of the techniques used by modern business concern for the purpose of cost reduction and cost control. The objective of standard costing is the same as that of budgetary control. The system involves a comparison of the actual with the standards and the discrepancy is called variance. The various steps involved in standard costing are as follows:

1. Setting of cost standards for various components of cost such as raw materials, labours and overheads. The standards fix the limit within which the different types of expenses must be kept.
2. Measurement of actual performance.
3. Comparison of actual cost with the standard cost laid down.
4. Finding the variance of actual cost from the standard cost.
5. Finding the cause of variance.
6. Taking necessary action to prevent the occurrence of variance in future.

5.9.1.3. Financial Statements and Ratio Analysis

The Trading Profit and Loss Account, the balance sheet of a company are the usual financial statements which are prepared ex post (in retrospect) to indicate what financial events occurred since the last statements. Depending on the company, the period covered by a financial statement could be the previous year, the previous quarter, or the previous month.

The usefulness of these statements for applying control measures is limited by the fact that they cover only post events. However, they can provide managers with useful information about trends. Managers can also use these statements to compare their organizations with other organization and can thus evaluate their own performance. In addition, they are used by people outside the organization to evaluate the organizations strength's, weakness and potential.

Ratio Analysis seeks to extract information from a financial statement in a way that will allow an organization's financial performance or condition to be evaluated. It involves selecting two significant figures from a financial statement and expressing their relationship in terms of a percentage or ratio.

The Ratios most commonly used by organizations are as follows:

1. *Liquidity Ratio:* They measure the company's ability to pay back short-term debts by converting assets quickly into cash. In other words, they are a measure of a company's

liquidity. One such ratio is the current ratio. It is expressed by the fraction: current assets + current liabilities.

2. *Debt Ratio:* While liquidity ratios are used to measure a company's short-term financial position, debt ratios are computed to assess its ability to meet long-term commitments. The simplest debt ratio is total debt divided by total assets. This ratio tells us what proportion of the company's assets is owned by its creditors.
3. *Profitability Ratio:* These ratios express as percentage of sales or of total depict the company's efficiency of operation. A profit of ₹ 4 lakhs, for example is unimpressive if it is derived from a total sales of ₹ 40 crores or a capital investment of ₹ 100 crores.
4. *Operating Ratio:* These ratios measure how efficiently the manufacturing and sales are being carried out. Some of the more common operating ratios are the inventory turnover ratio and the total assets turnover ratio. The inventory turnover ratio is defined as sales + inventory. It suggests that how the assets are being used efficiently by the firm.

The total assets turnover ratio is expressed as sales/total assets. This ratio gives an indication of how effectively the firm's assets are being used.

These ratio analysis comparisons can be made in one of two ways by comparisons over a time period. The present ratio compared with the same organization's ratio in the past: and comparison with other similar organization's or with the industry as a whole. The first type of comparison will indicate how the organization performance or condition has changed: the second type will suggest how well the organization is doing relative to its competitors.

5.9.1.4. Return on Investment

One particular approach to financial control that has received considerable attention in recent years is the return on investment ratio (ROI), also known as the Du Pont systems of financial analysis. It is expressed by the following formula:

$$ROI = Sales/Investment\ (Fixed\ and\ working\ capital) * profit/sales$$

This ratio is computed on the basis of capital turnover (sales/investment) multiplied by earnings as a proportion of sales (profit/sales). This calculation recognizes that one division, with a high capital turnover and a lower percentage of earnings to sales, may be more profitable in terms of return of investment than another with a high percentage of profits to sales but with low capital turnover.

5.9.1.5. Break-Even Analysis

Break-Even analysis is another control device used in business firms. It involves of a chart to depict the overall volume of sales necessary to cover costs. It is point which the cost and revenue of the enterprise are exactly equal. In other words, it is that point where the enterprise neither earns a profit nor incurs a loss.

Break-even analysis can be used both as an aid in decision-making and as a control device. The specific areas where break-even analysis can help in decision-making include.

1. Identifying the minimum sales volume necessary to prevent loss.

2. Identifying the minimum sales volume to meet established profit objectives.
3. Providing information helpful in making decision on the effect of raising or lowering prices, and
4. Providing data helpful in decisions to drop or add product lines.

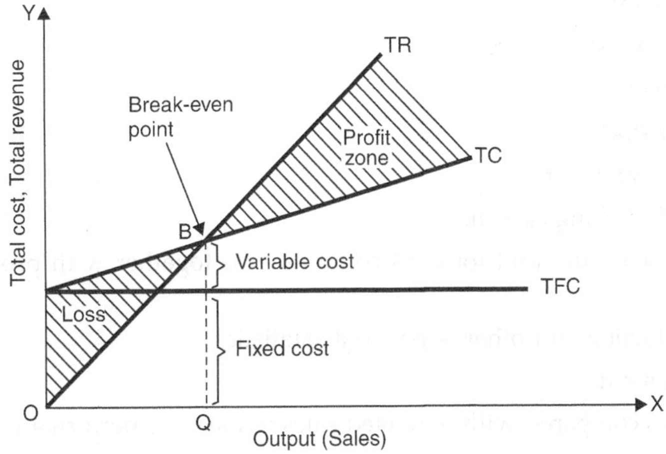

As an aid to control, break-even analysis provides one more yardstick by which to evaluate company's performance at the end of a sales period.

The break-even point can be calculated with the following formula

$$\text{Break-even point} = \frac{\text{Fixed costs}}{\text{Price} - \text{Variable Cost}}$$

$$\text{Break-even point} = \text{Price} - \text{Variable costs per unit}$$

5.9.1.6. Internal Audit and External Audit

Internal audit is another control techniques used by modern management. Internal audit is conducted by an internal auditor who is an employee of the organization. He makes an independent appraisal of financial and other operations. In addition, he appraises company's policies, plans and management performance. He pinpoints defects in the policies or plans and gives suggestions for eliminating the defects. As internal audit is conducted regularly, it keeps the employees always alert.

External audit is an independent appraisal of the organization financial accounts and statements. The purpose of external audit is to ensure that the interests of shareholders and other outside parties connected with the company are safeguard against the malpractices of the management. The external auditors is a qualified person and he has to certify the annual profit and loss account and balance sheet, carefully examination of the relevant books of accounts and documents. In case the external auditor is negligent in performing his duties or becomes party to any fraud or error committed by the management, he will be liable under both civil and criminal laws.

5.9.1.7. Reports

A major part of control consists of preparing reports to provide information to the management for purpose of control and planning. The following are certain types of reports which are prepared and submitted to the management regularly:

1. **Top Management**
   (*i*) Profit and loss statement.
   (*ii*) Balance sheet.
   (*iii*) Position of stock.
   (*iv*) Cash-flow statement.
   (*v*) Position of working capital.
   (*vi*) Capital expenditure and forward commitments together with progress of projects in hand.
   (*vii*) Sales, production and other appropriate statistics.
2. **Sales Management**
   (*i*) Actual sales compared with budgeted sales to measure performance by:
   (*a*) Products
   (*b*) Territories
   (*c*) Individual salesman
   (*d*) Customers.
   (*ii*) Standard Profit and Loss by a Product:
   (*a*) *For fixing selling prices and*
   (*b*) *To concentrate sales on most profitable products.*
   (*iii*) Selling expenses in relation to budget and sales value analyzed by
   (*a*) *Products*
   (*b*) *Territories*
   (*c*) *Individual salesman*
   (*d*) *Customers.*
   (*iv*) Bad debts and accounts, which are slow and difficult in collections.
   (*v*) Status reports on new or doubtful customers.
3. **Production Management**
   (*i*) *To Buyer:*
   - Price variations on purchase analyzed by commodities.

   (*ii*) *To Foreman:*
   - Operational efficiency for individual operators, duly summarized as department averages.
   - Labour utilization report and causes of lost time and controllable time.

- Indirect shop expenses against the standard allowed
- Scrap report.

(*iii*) *To Works Manager:*

- Department operating statement.
- General works operating statement (expenses relating to all works not directly allocable or controllable by departments).
- Plant utilization report.
- Department scrap report.
- Material usage report.

4. Special Reports

These reports may be prepared at the request of the management accountant or the manager. The necessity for them may arise on account of the need for a more detailed information on matters of interest first revealed by the routine reports. Some of the matters in respect of which such reports may be prepared are:

(*a*) Taxation, legislation and its effect on profit.

(*b*) Estimation about the earnings capacity of a new project.

(*c*) Break-Even analysis.

(*d*) Replacement of capital equipment.

(*e*) Special pricing analysis.

(*f*) Make or buy decision.

Some important considerations in drawing up these reports are as follows:

(*a*) ***Information Quality.*** The more accurate the information, the higher its quality and the more securely managers can rely on it when deciding what action to take. However, the cost of obtaining information increases as the quality of the information desired goes up. How accurate the information needs to be will vary with the situation. But in general, information of higher quality that does not add materially to a managers decision-making capability is not worth the added cost.

(*b*) ***Information Timeless.*** The information provided by a report must suggest action in time for that to be taken. Just when information is considered timely, however, will depend on situation. For example reports destined far top-level managers to monitor progress on long-range objectives may be considered timely if they aware at quarterly intervals. The cost of making them available weekly would not be justified, since long-range plans are neither reviewed nor modified at such frequent intervals. However, middle and lower level managers responsible for emerging operations and activities may need a weekly at even daily report on machine downtime if delays are to be minimized. The quality control managers must get a daily a weekly report on all customer rejections. On a monthly as quarterly basis, such information would merely be ancient history and would be of no value to the manager.

Timeliness may also be determined by company policy on by events, rather than by the calendar. Information on inventory, for example, is provided to the manager responsible for regarding only where a previously established minimum level for the inventory is being approached. Requiring inventory information on a calendar basis–such as away week. When inventory levels for most items are well a bore their record point would usually not be worth the added cost, since action would not be implied by the information.

(c) ***Information Quantity and Relevance.*** A report that provides too little information cash be ineffective, because it may lead managers to make wrong at late decisions that worsen problems instead of solving them conversely a report that provides managers too much information can also provide ineffective because that may not isolate what they need from a flood of irrelevant facts and figures. A good report should fill as evaluate information so that only the most relevant information is supplied to the appropriate manager. In addition, a good report should condense information, so that what is relevant may be absorbed in a short period of time.

5.9.1.8. Standing Orders, Rules, Limitations

Standing orders, rules and limitations are also control techniques used by the management. The manager, who authorized his subordinate to make curtain decisions as delegates some of his powers, lays down the limits for them. Limits may be decided on the basis of the nature of work and status of the subordinate. The management issues standing orders and they are to be observed by the subordinates. They may be concerned with the rules, regulations, discipline, procedures, conditions, timings etc.

5.9.1.9. Personnel Observation

A manager can also exercise fruitful control over his subordinates by observing them while they are engaged in work. Personnel observations help the manager not only in knowing the worker's attitude towards but also in correcting their work and methods, if necessary. More over, when the worker knows that his superior is observing him, he will be alert and will not waste his time. But in some cases he may also upset being observed and may develop resistance. In any case, their method is very costly and cannot work in large concern any degree of accuracy.

5.10. MANAGEMENT BY OBJECTIVES (MBO)

5.10.1. Meaning of MBO

MBO is both philosophy and a technique of management. It represents a rational and systematic approach to management wherein measurable goals are set up in consultation with subordinate managers and the contribution of each individual is judged in terms of such goals.

5.10.2. Definition of MBO

"MBO is a process whereby the superior and the subordinate managers of an enterprise jointly identify its common goals, define each individual's major areas of responsibility in terms of the

results expected of him, and use these measures as guides for operating the unit and assessing the contribution of each of its members."

—George Odiorne

5.10.3. Objectives of MBO

Management by objectives is intended primarily:

1. To measure and judge performance.
2. To relate individual performance to organizational goals.
3. To clarify both the job to be done and the expectations of accomplishment.
4. To foster the increasing competence and growth of the subordinates.
5. To serve as a basis for judgements about salary and promotion.
6. To stimulate the subordinates' motivation; and
7. To serve as a device for organization control and integration.
8. To Serve as a device for organizational control and integration.

5.10.4 Features of MBO

1. MBO focuses attention on what must be accomplished (goals) rather than on how it is to be accomplished (methods). It is a goal-oriented rather than work-oriented approach.
2. MBO involves participation of subordinate managers in the goal setting process. It requires all key personnel to contribute maximum to achieve the overall objectives.
3. MBO stresses measurable and verifiable goals in key result areas. It attempts to blend and balance the goals of all key personnel.
4. MBO is a dynamic system, which seeks to integrate the company's need to achieve its objectives with the manager's need to contribute and develop himself.
5. MBO is an overall philosophy of management that allows management to attain maximum results from available resources. It is not a set of rules or procedures but a way of thinking about managing.
6. MBO has an operational thrust involving linkage between organizational goals and individual goals.
7. MBO is a continuous process of goal setting, periodic appraisals and modification of goals and performance.
8. It sets an evaluative mechanism by which the contribution of each individual can be measured.

5.10.5. Steps in MBO Process

1. ***Preliminary Goal-setting.*** The first phase of MBO is the clarification of the objectives which the organization is to attain. The long-term overall goals of the enterprise are laid down in the key result areas. These goals are laid down keeping in view the internal and external environments of the organization. These goals are preliminary and tentative

subject to modification as the full range of verifiable objectives is evolved by the organization. While the strategic objectives may be verbal, operational goals must be measurable so as to serve definite yardsticks of goals accomplishment.

2. *Fixing Key Result Areas (KRA).* Key Result Areas (KRAs) are identified on the basis of organizational objectives and planning premises. These are the areas reference to which organizational health can be measured. Key result areas are arranged on the priority basis. Some examples of KRAs are
   - Profitability
   - Market standing
   - Innovation
   - Productivity
   - Market performance
   - Public responsibility etc.

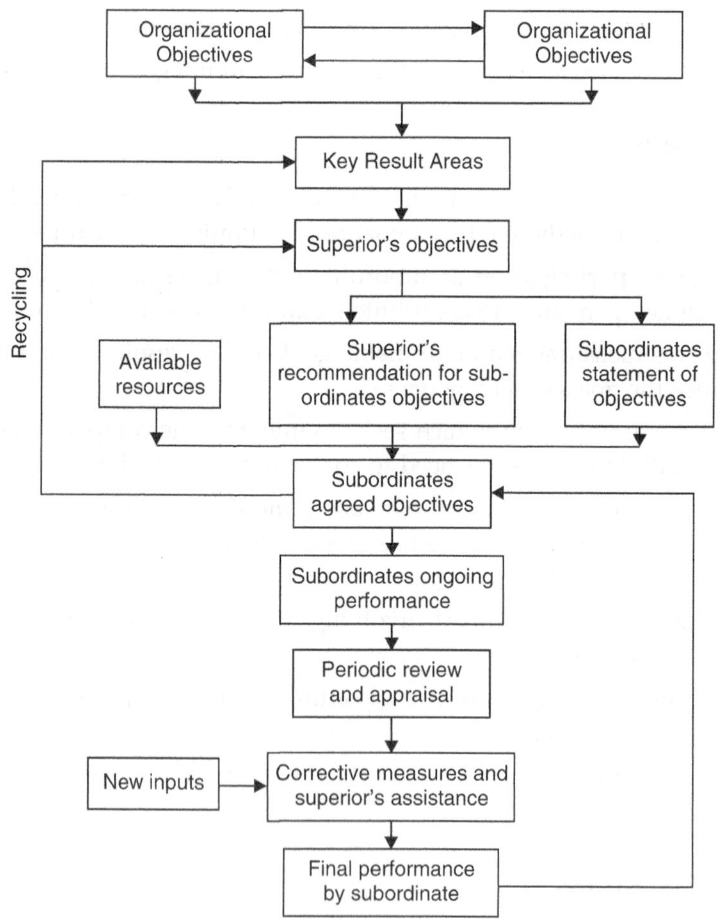

These areas may vary for different organization. KRAs indicate the strength of an organization.

3. *Setting Subordinates' Objectives.* The organizational objectives are achieved through individuals. Therefore, each individual must know what he is expected to achieve. In

setting objectives for subordinates, the organizational goals, subordinates' ability and resources available to him should be duly considered. Subordinates' objectives must be set in consultation with the individuals concerned. The allocation of resources should also be made in consultation with subordinates. There must be proper matching of goals and resources.

4. ***Recycling Objectives.*** Under MBO goals setting is not direction from the top management only. Rather it is a two-way process in which the superior suggests a goal that is acceptable to the subordinate. Goal setting is a joint and interactive process. A network of objectives is created so that every lower level objective contributes effectively to the achievement of the objectives next to it.
5. ***Action Planning.*** Once goals are established at all levels, action programmes are developed for their accomplishment. Detailed procedures are set up for their accomplishment. Detailed procedures are set up for the utilization of resources and for achievement for pre-determined targets. Action planning may call for revision of existing organization structure. The organization charts, manuals and job descriptions should be suitably amended. The authority and responsibility of each job and its relationship with other jobs should be clearly defined. Checkpoints should be established for evaluation of results in key areas.
6. ***Periodic Performance Reviews.*** At specified intervals, progress towards the accomplishment of goals is reviewed in consultation with subordinates. Such reviews are made to identify shortcomings and to take timely steps to improve results. Feedback from these reviews is provided to each individual to facilitate self-regulation and control. Progress towards the goal is discussed and potential for improvement is identified. In such reviews, the superior serves as a counselor and guide to the subordinates.
7. ***Final Appraisal.*** A thorough evaluation of performance is made at the end of the year. Achievements are analyzed in the light of established goals and standards. If a subordinate does not achieve their objectives, then the superior should identify what are the problems and how these problems can be overcome. The main purpose of the appraisal is to find out the shortcomings in achieving objectives and also to remove them promptly. Rewards are decided on the basis of such appraisal.

5.10.6. Advantages and Disadvantages of MBO

Sl.No.	Advantages of MBO	Disadvantages of MBO
1	Improved managerial performance.	Difficulty in goal setting.
2	Concentration of profit making activities.	Time consuming.
3	Better delegation.	More paper work.
4	Improved communication.	Pressure on people.
5	Improved morale and sense of purpose.	Leadership problems.
6	More effective development of executives.	
7	Early recognition of management potential.	

5.11. MANAGEMENT BY EXCEPTION (MBE)

One of the most important ways of tailoring controls for efficiency and effectiveness is to make sure that they are designed to point out exception. In other words, by concentrating on exceptions from planned performance, controls based on the time-honored exception principle to allow managers to detect those places where their attention is required and should be given. This implies the use of management by exception particularly in controlling aspect. Management by exception is a system of identification and communication the signals to the manager when his attention is needed.

Management by exception has six basic ingredients: Measurement, projection, selection, observation, comparison and decision-making.

(*i*) Measurement assigns values to past and present performances. This is necessary because without measurement of some kind, it would be impossible to identify an exception.

(*ii*) Project analyses those measurements that are meaningful to organizational objectives and extends them into future expectations.

(*iii*) Selection involves the criteria which management will use to follow progress towards organizational objectives.

(*iv*) Observation state of management by exception involves measurement of current performance so that managers are aware of the current state of affairs in the organization.

(*v*) Comparison stage makes comparison of actual and planned performances and identifies the exceptions that require attention and reports the variances to the management.

(*vi*) Decision-making prescribes the action that must be taken in order to bring performance back into control or to adjust expectations to reflect changing conditions or to exploit opportunity.

However, the major difference lies in the fact that the superior's attention is drawn in the case of exceptional differences between planned performance and actual performance. In other cases, subordinate manager takes decisions. However, what is exceptional requires the completion of whole process.

Benefits of Management by Exception

Management by Exception saves executives time because they apply themselves on fewer problems, which are important. Other details of the problems are left to the subordinates.

Instead of spreading managerial attention across all sorts of problems, it is placed selectively where and when it is needed. Thus it ensures better utilization of managerial talents.

MBE facilitates better delegation of authority, increases span of management and consequently provides better opportunities of self-motivational personnel in the organization.

Management by exception makes better use of knowledge of trends, history and available business data. It forces managers to review past history and to study related business data because these are the foundations upon which standards are derived and from which exceptions are noted.

It helps in identification of crises at the moment in which any exceptional deviation occurs; the attention of higher-level manager is drawn. In this way, it alerts management about their opportunities and difficulties.

Management by exception provides qualitative and quantitative yardsticks for judging situations and people.

It enhances the degree of communication between different segments of an organization. With its focus on results, it seeks to relate causes, regardless of their place in the organization, with overall organizational results. As such it encourages exchange of information between functions and also between a function and cost centre or profit centre to which it reports.

5.12. NEW CONTROL TECHNIQUES

These techniques which are of recent origin also not markedly overlap the traditional control devices, but provide the kind of information not readily available with the traditional methods. Therefore, when these control techniques are used, it is usually in addition to the control devices described in the preceding section.

5.12.1. PERT and CPM

The two major techniques under this heading are PERT (Programme Evaluation and Review Technique) and CPM (Critical Path Method). Both Techniques were developed independently, although virtually at the same time, around 1957-58. PERT was first developed for the US navy in connection with the Polaris weapon system and is credited with reducing the completion time of the programme by two years. CPM was developed jointly by Du Pont and Remington Rand of USA in order to facilitate the control of large, complex industrial projects.

Both PERT and CPM are primarily oriented towards achieving better managerial control of time spent in completing a project. Under both the techniques, a project is decomposed into activities and then all activities are integrated in a highly logical sequence to find the shortest time required to complete the entire project. The main difference between PERT and CPM lies in the treatment of time estimates. PERT was created primarily to handle research and development projects in which time spans are hard to estimate with any degree of accuracy, consequently, PERT time span are based on probabilistic estimates. CPM, on the other hand, is usually concerned with projects that the organisation has had some previous experience with time estimates, therefore, can be made relatively accurately.

The use of both PERT and CPM has spread rapidly today in controlling time-critical projects such as reinforcing a weak class, constructing a building at an olympic site as completing contracts that include penalty payment clauses. Many companies, make use of three techniques for working out the cost estimates of a project also.

5.12.2 Steps Involved in Developing the Network

Both under PERT and CPM, the purpose is to divide the project into a number of operations and then to draw a picture of the order in which and of the time when these operations should be started and completed. This picture is known as the project graph or arrow diagram. The following steps are involved in drawing this diagram.

1. The first step is to break down the whole project into a number of clearly identifiable activities and event. An activity is the actual performance of a task. The preceding event is called the 'tail event' and the following is called 'head event'.
2. Once the list of various activities is ready, we have to examine each activity in relation to the other activity.
3. The next step is to draw the diagram portraying the precedence, concurrence and subsequence of all activities and events. On this diagram, arrows show all activities and circles show all events. In CPM diagrams, a single time estimate is written against each activity. In PERT, each activity is assigned three time estimates.
   (*i*) **Optimistic.** Shortest time the activity takes place.
   (*ii*) **Most likely.** Time is estimated under practical situations, in which certain things go wrong and some go as per plan.
   (*iii*) **Pessimistic.** Longest time the activity takes place.

   Generally the three estimates for each activity are combined into a weighted average, called expected activity time.
4. Finally, the critical path is determined. The critical path is the longest path through the network in terms of amount of time the entire project will take. It indicates a series of activities which must be done in sequence and which will take longer than the other sequence of jobs that can go along simultaneously. It is critical because the time spent on the activities that lies along this path must be shortened if the total time of project is to be shortened.

5.12.3. Uses of PERT and CPM

1. It ensures actual planning.
2. It makes every manager fully aware of his responsibility.
3. It ensures improved management of resources.
4. It facilitates future-oriented control.
5. It facilitates improved decision-making.
6. It ensures simultaneous performance of different parts of work.

5.12.4. Limitations of PERT and CPM

1. They are suitable mainly in cases where time is the essence of performance or where cost and time are so related that by controlling time, cost is controlled.
2. Estimate of time, cost and events are seldom available with the precision required for effective control through PERT. Errors in estimate of the numerous inter locking points of the chart may add up to a situation to make the PERT chart erratic and unreliable as a control technique.
3. PERT has a limited application to one time non-repetitive projects. It does not help control in continuous processing and production.

INDEX

Q

R

S

T

U

V

X

Y

Z